THE
CULTURAL
CHURCH

THE CULTURAL CHURCH

F. LaGard Smith

20th Century Christian

2809 GRANNY WHITE PIKE • NASHVILLE, TN 37204

ISBN 0-89098-131-0

To all those who share with me a rich spiritual heritage in the churches of Christ—

Who, more importantly, are children of God through Christ Jesus and heirs according to the promise.

With Appreciation

More than any other book I have written, this book has been through a crucible of fire, tested by those whose opinions I greatly respect. It should be said that none of them would completely agree with everything presented herein. In fact, several were chosen because they have significantly different perspectives. For their personal faith, keen scholarship, and uncompromising candor, I thank them all: Tony Coffey, Stephen Givens, Kregg Hood, Jerry Jones (Oxford), Howard Norton, Tom Olbricht, Rubel Shelly, Tim Woodroof, and Jerry Yarbrough.

With special appreciation to Jim Bury, whose mind and heart have touched this book to make it what it could not otherwise have been.

CONTENTS

Part One

THE THORNY PROBLEM OF INTERPRETING THE BIBLE

Some Folks Call It "Hermeneutics"

Religion is as necessary to reason as reason is to religion. The one cannot exist without the other.
– George Washington

ONE

At The Crossroads

As if Religion were intended
For nothing else but to be mended.
Samuel Butler: Hudibras,
Pt. I, Canto I, l. 205

Our fellowship is having an identity crisis. In some respects, it is not a bad thing. Identity crises are times of self-scrutiny and reassessment which can lead to much-needed mid-course corrections and renewed vitality. The only alternative to periodic introspection is blind traditionalism and stagnation.

On a variety of fronts, many are beginning to ask if we've given enough attention to the "weightier matters" of love, justice, discipleship, the Spirit, servanthood, and a host of other biblical concerns that are at the heart of a Christ-centered life. Have we been primarily concerned with doctrine relating to church organization and function and not sufficiently concerned with doctrine relating to the cross of Christ? Have we allowed ourselves to get entrenched in forms and rituals which limit our individual spiritual growth? More and more among us are beginning to think so.

Conscientious, Bible-believing Christians throughout the churches of Christ are beginning to ask hard questions about our traditional approach to worship and study. They don't want to follow blindly along a familiar path if it means missing the core message of Christ. In that desire, they have caught the true spirit of restoration—trying to get back to basics, trying to make sure that no outer forms stand in the way of our being simply Christians.

Change is in the wind, and in many ways it's a refreshing breeze for the better. But from other quite unexpected directions there is also an ill wind blowing. As if Satan sensed the spirit of revival, there is a growing threat among our fellowship of change being demanded for wrong reasons, of calls for radical shifts based on unworthy considerations. Along with those who are trying to scale the barriers of traditionalism in order to better know God, Christ, and the Holy Spirit, there are also those who are trying to find in the Bible a rationalization for doing what the Bible simply won't allow.

The irony is that we ourselves may not always know which category we are in. God puts the church in culture and asks us to be an influence for good. Sometimes we lose sight of our mission and end up being the very ones who are changed! Instead of permeating culture with the fragrance of Christ, or being counter-culture where necessary, we ourselves become captive to culture. So much so, that we hardly recognize it when it happens. So much so, that we don't even realize that we've begun to read the Bible through the lens of culture rather than through the lens of faith.

Our current identity crisis may be the result of honest self-scrutiny and a sincere desire for spiritual renewal. Or it may merely reflect the extent to which we are the products of our own generation and the spirit of the age. Indeed, there may be a combination of influences at work. Satan is more than clever in leading us astray. He knows that legitimate concerns can open the door to less worthy conclusions.

The first premise of this book is that the church is at great risk of becoming a cultural church. By that I mean a church succumbing to a culture which in the last two decades has radically changed the way it sees the world and even the way it thinks. Without our realizing it, we can become caught up in a secular mindset that has little regard for the authority of God's revelation. So subtle is the change in our thinking, that we may not even recognize how far removed we are from where we started, nor how great a threat to faith our new thinking has become.

The second premise of the book is that recent calls for a "new hermeneutic" may reflect that cultural influence more than any of us are prepared to admit. To the extent that such calls reflect a culture-charmed church, there is the danger of confusing valid concerns with less-noble motivations which are constantly at work within us.

Herman Who?

The mere mention of the word *hermeneutics* will already have been too great a jump for many readers. *Hermeneutics* is a word that has captured the attention of church scholars in recent years, but may not be familiar to others. Being as non-technical as possible, what *hermeneutics* means for our purpose is the method by which we either understand the original intent of the Scriptures or, more to the point of recent controversy, how we decide which things we read about in the Bible are important for us to practice as Christians today.

Hermeneutics, for example, might be about whether we should "greet one another with a holy kiss," as the Corinthians were encouraged to do; or whether women should "remain silent" as Paul instructed Christian women in the first century; or whether we have any biblical authority one way or the other regarding the use of instruments in our worship. In short, hermeneutics is our method of interpreting and applying Scripture.

The call for a "new hermeneutic" necessarily infers that there is an "old hermeneutic" in need of replacement. Many of us involved in the controversy over hermeneutics assume that everyone is familiar with that "old hermeneutic." To the question, "How are we to understand Scripture?" the answer has been given, "By command, example, and necessary inference." But hardly anyone I talk to today (especially among younger Christians) has the slightest clue about what was once a widely understood concept in our fellowship.

The fact that so few people in our fellowship today have even heard of "command, example, and necessary inference" is its own telling commentary. It suggests 1) how far we have come from our roots and 2) how difficult it may be to attach much blame to it for our current concerns.

Under "the old hermeneutic," the goal has been to imitate whatever practices we find in Scripture in the form of either direct "commands," biblical "examples," or any other "necessary inferences" which might flow therefrom. The idea has been that, if we faithfully pattern our own Christian walk on biblical commands and examples, then we can be the same kind of Christians—worshipping God in the same way—as Jesus' disciples in the first century.

The Call for a New Hermeneutic

What lies behind the call for a new hermeneutic is not always easy to grasp. Sometimes, it is a label that is put on a wide-ranging list of concerns loosely associated with perceived abuses of the "old hermeneutic." These concerns range from scriptures taken out of context, to an overemphasis on church organization and function, to the need for expressing greater spirituality in our lives and in our mutual worship together.

Sometimes, the call is not for any single, comprehensive "new hermeneutic," but for a whole array of individual hermeneutics, each specially tailored to help us interpret a particular type of biblical literature. It is the concern particularly of our Christian scholars that we have often run roughshod over any number of passages because we have not stopped long enough to do our homework. Their fear is that we have tried to put poetry, prophecy, law, and gospel all into the same cookie cutter, when our cookie cutter (the "old hermeneutic") was not designed for those particular batches of theological dough.

If only that could summarize the issue. Unfortunately, however, it appears that the call for a new hermeneutic has a very real potential for not only getting rid of the "old hermeneutic" but, more particularly, the authority of Scripture which it represents. It is here that we encounter the cultural church, and here that we face our greatest threat. (Even legitimate criticism of the "old hermeneutic" has already been hijacked by some to provide support for less worthy purposes.)

While both recognizing and honoring more legitimate concerns regarding how we are to understand Scripture, the focus of this book is on the seduction of those who have been caught up (unwittingly, for the most part) in a culture which elevates one's own intuitive self-direction over a rational pursuit of God's truth as found in divine revelation. This book is meant to be a window to a radically changed world around us and a mirror of the insidious imprint it can have on all of us.

Even the sound of the word *hermeneutics* reminds me of some fancy name a doctor might use to describe a nasty skin condition. But like a painful rash which might be caused by, say, some dietary deficiency, the battle over hermeneutics not only asks a more fundamental question (What constitutes biblical authority?) but also may be merely symptomatic of a changing culture which is bringing these questions to the fore. This book seeks to point out what may be unrecognized forces behind much of our current discontent—causes that promise, even in the immediate future, to affect all of us in the church, whether or not we can even spell the word *hermeneutics.*

Advance Apologies and Other Disclaimers

Lest this book be seen to tar with the same brush every motivation, worthy and unworthy, behind the call for a new hermeneutic, let me say up front that I wish only to signal a warning against the enticing spirit of the cultural church. It is a ruthless spirit which can hold captive even the sincerest among us, and deceive us at the very moment of greater commitment.

"The cultural church," as I use the term, is a *mindset* or a *particular perspective*, not specific individuals who could be identified or a particular congregation here or there. It may prove to be a frustration to some readers, but I have studiously avoided further defining "the cultural church," lest the book appear to be more accusatorial than it may already sound.

Early on in the writing of this book, I made a conscious decision which I may yet live to regret. I decided not to quote from any current writers or scholars among our fellowship, for fear that the book might thereby become person-oriented rather than issue-oriented. Having grown up in a hostile climate of personality assassination within the church, I abhor the very thought and want no part of it.

A second consideration is equally important. Although I

happen to disagree with various authors and scholars on the particular issues addressed in this book, I have no desire to tarnish their efforts to express important concerns on other matters which need to be brought to our attention. Some excellent thinking and writing is going on in our fellowship these days, with a collegial spirit far superior to what we have often witnessed in the past. If there are points of serious disagreement, or matters warranting extreme caution, these must not be permitted to cloud the bigger picture.

Unfortunately, I am already painfully aware that my decision to talk about issues without providing specific examples of *who* has said *what* has weakened my arguments in the eyes of some. (My reviewers are already demanding more evidence.) However, I can assure you that "the cultural church" is no straw man. I have read widely among the literature coming out of our fellowship over the past several years and am convinced that, among many in the church today, there is more to the call for a new hermeneutic than always meets the eye. The evidence lies in any number of scholarly papers and books which at this moment are within easy reach on my desk.

If my response to the wide-ranging hermeneutics discussion among us seems to put too many people in the same bed, I'm afraid it's because there is already a blurring of lines between proper and improper reasons being urged for getting rid of "the old hermeneutic." I sense that there is a "second generation" of new-hermeneutics advocates who have run far beyond the "first generation's" more considered concerns. It's all the difference between those who honor the authority of Scripture and therefore want to better facilitate our understanding of it, and those who have given up on the authority of Scripture. My fear is that even those who have not themselves proceeded from the mindset of "the cultural church" risk the further fostering of that very mindset through some of the approaches they are offering as alternatives to "the old hermeneutic."

What may also confuse (perhaps anger) some readers is my attempt to answer a wide divergence of opinion coming out of the hermeneutics controversy. Even among those of my reviewers who generally agree on the need for a new hermeneutic, I'm getting radically different feedback. Some support a more narrative-style hermeneutic, while others say they have never even heard of it! Some interpret John Locke (whom we will introduce in a later chapter) in one way, while others see him in an entirely different light. The end result is that this book will be many things to many different people. (Is that because we each begin with our own *personal* hermeneutic?)

For that reason, the reader who says "I've got real problems with 'the old hermeneutic,' but what this book describes as 'new hermeneutic' thinking certainly doesn't describe *my* thinking," will be in good company. (And I know of *no one* who wants to be associated with the kind of New Age world view that I strongly suggest is working its way into our thinking.) As a kind of reassuring balance, it should also be said that my more conservative reviewers have been equally disturbed at various points along the way.

Writing tailor-made books corresponding to each reader's perspective is obviously impossible. Rather than attempting to sort out proper from improper concerns in each instance, I have tried to focus on a common enemy—a revolutionary cultural mindset which threatens to consume us all.

Frankly, if no discussion of hermeneutics whatever had proceeded the writing of this book, that discussion would have happened sooner or later. I suspect sooner. How we view Scripture cannot help but be affected by the radical changes now taking place in cultural thinking. Our current discussion will seem like child's play compared with what we will soon be hearing from today's youth. It is not only for us, but for them, that this book goes out.

Overview of the Book

By way of introduction to what follows, it is important to see this book in three distinct parts. In the remainder of Part One, we will explore the background of the so-called "old hermeneutic," and evaluate its effectiveness in bringing about a proper understanding of Scripture. There will be much to commend but also some aspects to question. Chapter Two, containing a lifetime of reminiscences from my own experience in the church, is my attempt to personalize some of the more abstract issues that confront us as a fellowship. It will be an opportunity for each reader to reflect back on his or her own experience, aware of how our individual backgrounds may color our thinking on current issues.

In Chapter Three, I pay tribute to the so-called "old hermeneutic" for the commendable way in which it represents our fellowship's commitment to biblical authority. Unlike creeds, which formalize particular doctrinal understanding, our hermeneutic has always called us back to the written Word itself. Chapter Four begins with an introspective look at the churches of Christ and how our heritage of countering denominationalism has shaped our focus in some surprising ways. Among other things, we will explore the unusual emphasis we have given to *verse* in our attempt to honor "book, chapter, and verse."

At the close of the first section, Chapter Five points us to the revolutionary moral and social questions facing the church today. It's no longer drinking, dancing, and "mixed bathing" that our hermeneutic must deal with, but such tough issues as abortion, euthanasia, and surrogate parenting. Is "the old hermeneutic" able to meet such a challenge?

Part Two traverses a wide terrain in order to demonstrate how radically different our culture has become over a period of only two short decades, and the subtle ways in which that transformation may well be affecting our view about something as apparently remote as how we go about understanding the Bible. We will go down a number of seemingly unrelated paths, all of which, in their own way, lead to a single destination. Many of the paths will have been unfamiliar territory to most of us. Some might even appear to be complete detours. But I trust that the end result will be well worth the journey.

As Part Two begins, Chapter Six introduces us to the so-called "new morality" which is not simply moral decline (immorality), but the denial that there is any such thing as "right" and "wrong" (amorality). We will also take a look at how the liberal lobby enforces this "new morality" through a kind of mind control known as "political correctness." The surprise is that the "new morality" has striking similarities to the cultural church's call for a new hermeneutic.

Chapter Seven takes us into the heart of today's New Age thinking. It's no longer simply about reincarnation, out-of-body experiences, and psychic "channeling." It's about a radical shift from rational thought to intuitive, experiential perception—again, a reflection of the mindset most associated with the cultural church.

In Chapter Eight, we will look outside of our own fellowship to see that the church is not the only group going through the throes of struggle over hermeneutics—the best proof yet that culture has a much stronger influence on the issues currently facing our fellowship than any of us would like to admit. Chapter Nine is a response to the increasingly popular charge that the "old hermeneutic" is a mathematics-like scientific formula, modeled after the thinking of seventeenth-century philosopher John Locke and Enlightenment rationalism—and thus spiritually unworthy. (If that sounds a bit too scholarly, I promise an easy way out!)

Finally, Chapter Ten focuses on the idea of "narrative" as a new hermeneutic, pointing to both its strengths and weaknesses. Can seeing Scripture as "story," as some have suggested, help us to get a better handle on its core message, or does it lead us to a more slippery, subjective view of the Bible?

Part Three leaves the cultural church behind, concentrating directly on hermeneutics and how we can best understand the Bible for today. Even though Chapter Eleven comes near the end of the book, it is intended to be a central focus of our discussion. Chapter Eleven presents for consideration what I propose to be a *not-so-new* hermeneutic, summarized as "purpose, principle, and precedent." It is an attempt to provide an umbrella hermeneutic that will accommodate our need to interpret the many different forms of literature found in the Bible (whether law, poetry, prophecy, Gospels, or Epistles) while retaining the commendable features of "command, example, and necessary inference."

Chapter Twelve is devoted to *applying* "purpose, principle, and precedent" with a view toward better evaluating its practical implementation. We will also take a close look at the many inventive ways in which we manage to "overrule," or sidestep, any biblical guidelines that run counter to our thinking. In Chapter Thirteen, we explore the authority of scriptural silence, focusing particularly on the issue of instrumental music.   Under what circumstances is the silence of Scripture as important as specific biblical directives?

Finally, Chapter Fourteen wraps up the book with a challenge for us to be a church *in* culture without being a church *held captive* by culture.   In view of our rapidly changing world, how can we maintain cultural relevance while continuing to honor God through obedience to his Word?

The church on the brink of the twenty-first century stands at a pivotal moment in history. As Christians who live on the cutting edge of a brave new world, we must stretch our thinking like never before. Tired rhetoric will no longer win the day; nor dead traditionalism; nor an enthusiastic infusion of the world's standards. "Back to the Bible" is still the right call, and back to the God of the Bible an even greater challenge—especially for the cultural church.

TWO

When Hermeneutics First Hit Home

In politics, as in religion, we have less charity for those who believe the half of our creed, than for those who deny the whole of it.
— Charles Caleb Colton

From my earliest days, sitting on my mother's lap and listening to my father preach the gospel from the pulpit, I was weaned on phrases like "book, chapter, and verse" and "command, example, and necessary inference." It was my inherited initiation into a "back to the Bible" fellowship which called the religious world to "speak where the Bible speaks, and be silent where the Bible is silent." The Restoration Movement from which our fellowship had sprung was all about restoring New Testament Christianity, and how else could that be accomplished but by returning to the "pattern of sound teaching"[1] and "the faith that was once for all entrusted to the saints"?[2]

As a young man, I simply took for granted the authority of Scripture in determining the work and worship of the church. Even to my adolescent thinking, human creeds and traditions were anathema. Was it not human invention that had always led God's people astray? Bible class lessons drove home the point, from the golden calf at Sinai[3] to Uzzah's death when the ark of the covenant was mishandled;[4] from the unauthorized fire of Nadab and Abihu[5] to the burdensome rules of the Pharisees which Jesus condemned.[6]

If I did not yet know the history of western civilization, I knew the history of how the Roman Catholic Church had heretically evolved from first century Christianity, and how the Protestant denominations had attempted to reform Catholicism without achieving a restoration of the early church in its full doctrinal purity. Long before I was baptized, I already knew it was only the Church of Christ that I wanted to be a part of. Out of all the churches across the land, it was only the Church of Christ that respected God enough to obey his Word completely in matters of doctrine. We had no creed of our own. We did "Bible things in Bible ways." Ours was the legacy of Truth.   Indeed, the church was "the pillar and foundation of the Truth."[7]

A Shocking Introduction

At the impressionable age of twelve, youthful naivete regarding biblical interpretation and Christian attitudes in the wake of disagreements was shattered by an incident which, in contrast to the blur of youthful years now long forgotten, sticks irrevocably in my mind. It was a Sunday afternoon in Tulsa, Oklahoma. Several families from our congregation had come over to the house for what seemed like a wake for the dead. My father was crying. If I had ever seen him crying before, I hadn't remembered it. It took some time for everything to sink in, but eventually I came to understand that Dad had just been fired as preacher for our congregation. His crime? Preaching a sermon that morning in which he took a stand against what he felt to be an unbiblical practice relative to the work and organization of the church.

For a twelve-year-old more interested in Hopalong Cassidy and little league baseball than the finer points of church organization, Dad's particular understanding of "command, example, and necessary inference" regarding a specific doctrinal issue meant having to hurriedly vacate our church-owned house and move back to Texas. All I knew was that, because of some barely-pronounceable word called "hermeneutics," I would no longer play for the Washington Senators, and might never again see my fifth-grade sweetheart. Under such circumstances, even a young man begins to wonder just what all the fuss is about. Should a particular method of understanding, interpreting, and applying Scripture make such an important difference in one's life?

Early Thoughts About Church Unity

One observation came home to me fairly quickly. I knew that, if asked, the men who had called for Dad's firing would have said they too believed in "command, example, and necessary inference" as a method of determining church doctrine. It was not lost on even a twelve-year-old trying desperately to understand the mysteries of church politics that our plea for unity based upon a respect for Scripture was never as easily achievable as we pretended. If our "hermeneutic" was correct, then why couldn't those of us in the church who shared the same way of understanding the Bible easily agree as to what God was telling us through his Word? Yet whether outside the church or within, controversies still raged over issue after issue.

Far from achieving unity, our dogged determination to follow the authority of Scripture led to the acrimonious division of one congregation after another. A wave of disfellowshipping swept over the brotherhood. There were fellowships within fellowships; "your camp" and "mine"; the "liberals" and the "conservatives." Church papers spewed out invectives directed to this brother or that who happened to disagree on some nuance of doctrine.

Of course, one editor's "nuance" was another's "blasphemy." On each side, "matters of opinion" (about which we could disagree as brothers and sisters in Christ) had to yield to "matters of faith" (over which we were forced to divide). Naturally, the issues *we* thought to be crucial were "matters of faith" (with which everyone else had to agree), whereas the belief of anyone who disagreed with us was curtly dismissed as simply a "matter of opinion" (which could be ignored).

Even the college that I later chose to attend was distinguished by its stalwart doctrinal stand on certain rather esoteric, if significant, issues. It alone stood for Truth. Other church-related colleges had gone the way of all flesh—to unbridled liberalism. It hardly mattered that the other Christian colleges also taught "command, example, and necessary inference" as the proper way to understand and apply Scripture. When that commonly-shared formula of interpretation happened to yield different doctrinal conclusions, it was unforgivable doctrinal error.

The consequences were quite unbelievable. Those who promoted the error could no longer be fellowshipped. They were "erring Christians," a not-so-subtle euphemism meaning *second-class Christians* and (if we were really honest about it) only a fine line away from *not really being Christians at all!* Anyone who differed in his understanding of Scripture was automatically a "false teacher," so how could he possibly be fellowshipped as a true Christian? Given a choice between an "erring Christian" and someone else, we'd rather have lunch with social acquaintances who professed no belief whatsoever in God and his revealed Word, much less in our shared hermeneutic of "command, example, and necessary inference."

Being Honest About Inconsistency

If during my college years I was a loyal member of the "true remnant" of the church, I was not uncritical of my own understanding of Scripture. I began to see that my use of "command, example, and necessary inference" was shadowy, if not actually inconsistent. Like others, I took a somewhat smorgasbord approach to New Testament "commands." Why, for example, did I insist that Christ's command to the apostles to "go and make disciples of all nations"[8] was equally applicable to me as an evangelistic imperative, but that Paul's command to the Corinthians to "greet one another with a holy kiss"[9] was (as for the *kiss*, at least) culturally unique and therefore not applicable to me?

Particularly worrisome to me was the use of 1 Corinthians 16:2 in relation to the weekly collection. I wondered about our time-honored introduction to that collection: "We will now take this opportunity to lay by in store as we've been commanded to do on the first day of the week." Had *we* really been "commanded" to give of our means each Lord's day? Was taking up the collection really one of five mandatory "items of worship" (as it was taught in standard Bible class material), to be omitted only at our spiritual peril? Was our offering *commanded* in the same way as the Jewish tithe? Or, in fact, were Paul's instructions to the Corinthians directed simply at expediting a special offering for the poor saints in Jerusalem which the Corinthians themselves had initiated out of love for their struggling brethren?

And what about the selectivity with which I approached New Testament "examples"? Why did I feel comfortable with the weekly practice of observing *the Lord's Supper*—based upon only minimal textual reference[10]—while blithely ignoring the multiple references to *fasting*[11] and giving little credence to one example after another of the *laying on of hands*?[12] On what basis had I distinguished between certain examples which were "binding" and other examples which could be ignored as either "cultural" or merely "coincidental"? Command, example, and—more nebulous yet—"necessary inference" seemed more suited to perpetuating traditional church practices than to achieving biblical consistency.

Toward a More Spiritual Hermeneutic

And yet I was content to live with the ambiguity. I was comfortable in the knowledge that, "on the whole," we in the church were following the New Testament pattern as closely as anyone could. If we erred in some detail, at least we had caught the spirit of New Testament Christianity. *Hadn't we?* Or had we? It was not long before I was less comfortable with even that thought. Perhaps through "command, example, and necessary inference" we had substantially caught the *forms* of first century faith and practice, but I began to wonder whether we had actually caught the *spirit.*

As part of the most conservative stream within the church (the non-cooperation or anti-institutional congregations, as they were variously known), I had always resented the label "legalist." If it was *law* I was following, nevertheless it was *God's law*! All I could see in those whom we called "liberals" was a kind of soppy, all-is-love lip service to Scripture. With the "liberals" it was the *spirit* that counted, not *doctrine.* For my money, *spirit* was just a smokescreen for doing whatever you wanted to do, regardless of what Scripture might have to say.

However, my appreciation for having a greater spiritual life in Christ—over and above maintaining doctrinal purity—finally began to evolve, if ever so slowly.   As much as anything, I think my personal growth began out of a reaction to how I was treated when I dared to ask aloud the questions I had asked in the privacy of my own thoughts. Instead of being joined in a loving search for the truth (which we had always proclaimed loudly from the pulpit as our highest goal), all I got was an unloving "how-dare-you!" Whatever happened to the "nobility" of the Bereans who diligently searched the Scriptures?[13]   In my honest search for truth with my own brothers and sisters in Christ, I experienced neither nobility nor love.

It was then that I discovered there were other strugglers within the church—Christians whom, from a righteous distance, I had always dismissed as "liberals"; Christians with whom I had been warned not to fellowship.   But how differently it turned out. If they were "liberal," at least they allowed me to ask the questions that a more narrow fellowship would not permit me to ask.

And what a grand irony! Those who prided themselves in having the "right doctrine" were not secure enough to allow even the slightest challenge to that doctrine; while those whom I had always seen as taking doctrine far less seriously were open to a broader, more searching discourse. To my surprise, I found that I could actually be more "conservative" among the "liberals" than I could be "conservative" among the "conservatives"! And, none to the delight of the "conservatives" (or to the "liberals" for that matter), the further irony is that—for stronger reasons than an inherited faith alone will allow—I have remained a "conservative" to this day.

Learning to appreciate more "liberal" Christians for their sense of freedom in Christ was a true blessing. Coming from a more black-and-white perspective, I had a lot of rough edges that needed to be honed. What a breath of fresh air it was to move away from an overemphasis on the Epistles (which allow us to focus on the *church*) to a greater emphasis on the Gospels (which force us to focus on *Jesus* who gave his life for the church). What a release to find more than tired ritual in worship!

If only that could be the happy ending to the story. Unfortunately, what I have since come to learn about many of my newfound brothers and sisters in the faith is that their *openness* often reflects the kind of *liberty-cum-license* of which I was initially suspicious.   If they are open to unobstructed discourse about Scripture (usually at the initiation of someone else who happens to be so inclined), too often it is because they do not take Scripture as seriously as they ought.   At times they remind me of the philosophers on Mars Hill—willing to *listen* to anything, but willing to *commit* to nothing.[14] For them, biblical doctrine is "interesting" but not "compelling"; "directive," perhaps, but not "deciding."   For many "liberals," hermeneutics is just one more thing to be *free of* in their pursuit of spirit-filled living.

Of course, I need tell no one that the labels "conservative" and "liberal" are almost without meaning. "Conservative"— on what issue? "Liberal"—in comparison to whom? As you may already have gathered from these opening personal reflections, my own experience in the church has mostly been at the extremes of our fellowship—with the extremely conservative and the extremely liberal.   You may never have experienced either extreme.

Yet there can be no doubt that application of our traditional hermeneutic has made "liberals" and "conservatives" out of all of us at one time or another. And time and again, much to our shame, our abuse of "command, example, and necessary inference" has been our very undoing as a fellowship of believers.

Where to Turn?

If that is true, of course, the next question is obvious. What should we do with the "old hermeneutic"? Should we throw it out and start over again? That's the suggestion of many in the church today who are calling for a "new hermeneutic."   In truth, no single "new hermeneutic" has been proposed. Rather than one "unifying" hermeneutic to replace the old, what is being suggested are a number of new approaches which, taken individually or together, are said to give us a better handle on interpreting Scripture. For some in the cultural church, unfortunately, the call for something *new* is apparently only a frenzy for banishment of the *old*.

Would a new hermeneutic or a wide-ranging set of such guidelines eliminate the divisions among us? If we dropped the formula of "command, example, and necessary inference," would it bring an end to the ferocious infighting between "liberals" and "conservatives"? Would it keep some other twelve-year-old from having to leave his friends under a cloud of doctrinal controversy in which his parents were involved?

If I thought a "new hermeneutic" could do all of that, I'd be the first to welcome it! But who among us would ever believe that such total harmony could ever be achieved? Even without our current catch-phrase, "command, example, and necessary inference," apostle-guided Christians in the first century church had vexing problems of their own. How could we possibly devise the perfect way of understanding the Bible when dispute about the meaning and application of God's Word goes all the way back to the very first "command" of God in the Garden of Eden?[15]

Maybe that's our first clue. If disagreement over interpretation and application is as old as the ages, perhaps the problem lies somewhere other than in the particular *method* we might happen to use. Methods come and methods go, but still the difficulties remain. On the other hand, who would dare suggest that *just any* method will do, or that no one method is any better or worse than any other?

Given the inability of our traditional hermeneutic to achieve complete unity in doctrinal belief, perhaps there *is* room for improvement, or even room for something altogether new. In either case, surely, our aim will continue to be frustrated by the one factor which haunts all attempts at formulating a perfect biblical hermeneutic. That, of course, is the human factor. *You and I!* You and I and our deep longing to rest secure in the grip of the familiar. (Call it traditionalism if we must.) You and I and our hidden agendas. You and I and our penchant for using Scripture as a means of validating what we want to do in the first place. You and I and our way of reading the Bible which conveniently permits us to avoid the central, convicting message of God's revelation: Christ crucified!

What we need is a way of understanding the Bible that calls us higher. A hermeneutic that leads us away from Self and into the mind of God is a hermeneutic born of humility. A hermeneutic that robs us of unworthy motives and gives us a grand vision of what we could be with God's help is a hermeneutic worth fighting for. A hermeneutic which dares to be counter-culture when culture would lead us astray is a hermeneutic that can safeguard our eternal destiny when culture will have ceased to exist.

At the end of the day, the only question surely must be: How, by any means through the Scriptures, can we grasp the very essence of God and his will for our lives? If we must have a method of hermeneutics in order to answer those noble questions, then let it be a method which is—if not perfect—at least *worthy!*

THREE

In Praise Of The Old Hermeneutic

Precept begins, example accomplishes.
—French Proverb

A few years ago, a speaker at one of the Bible lectureships told about having been on a cross-country trip with several other brethren in an unmarked van. At some point along the way they were passed by another van which had "Church of Christ" painted on the side. Excited to know that there were kindred spirits on the road, the speaker and his fellow passengers waved wildly to catch the attention of the occupants in the van in front of them. They even honked, flicked the headlights, and drove up alongside the other van—all to no effect.

Suddenly, one of the passengers in the unmarked van had a stroke of brilliance and hurriedly drew a handscrawled sign with large letters which read, "ACTS 2:38!" That's all it took. The moment the driver of the other van saw the sign, he screeched to a halt and everybody got out and hugged each other like long-lost friends!

As the speaker pointed out, Acts 2:38 is *our scripture*! It *belongs* to the churches of Christ. We *own* it! It's such a hallmark of the church that we instantly recognize each other by its very mention. And why not? It's a wonderful passage reminding us of our response in faith to God's call and our baptism into Christ. It affirms that our sins are

forgiven according to the promise made on that great Pentecost day.

If perhaps as a fellowship of believers we have overworked
Acts 2:38, we have never inflated its actual value. It captures
magnificently the essence of man's obedient response to
God's merciful offer of grace. How, then, could it ever be
overstated! And what goes for Acts 2:38 goes also in some
respects for our characteristically-churches-of-Christ formulation of "command, example, and necessary inference."

As we shall see in later chapters, it is our *formulation* that
is characteristic of our fellowship, not the basic rules of
interpretation themselves. At various points in history, other
believers have caught a similar vision of biblical interpretation. In fact, we shall also see that the fundamental basis for
"our hermeneutic" is found in the New Testament itself, being
the very approach used by the apostles and Jesus himself in
interpreting Old Testament scriptures. If it is "ours," it is not
"ours alone."

It should also be noted that we have used the precise,
three-part formulation—"command, example, and necessary inference"—more in recent times than in the early years
of the restoration movement. Yet this widely-used formulation has its roots firmly planted in the very beginning of
restoration thought. In his *Declaration and Address* (1809),
Thomas Campbell pointedly referred to each of the three
parts of the more modern formulation:

> "...Nor ought anything to be admitted, as of
> Divine obligation, in their Church constitution
> and managements, but what is expressly en-
> joined by the authority of our Lord Jesus Christ
> and his apostles upon the New Testament
> Church; either in *express terms* or by *approved
> precedent.*"

> "...*Inferences* and deductions from Scrip-
> ture premises, when fairly inferred, may be truly
> called the doctrine of God's holy word...."[1]

We next see those hermeneutical elements in action when
Thomas and Alexander Campbell first struggled with infant

baptism. Gradually, they came to realize that neither "express terms" nor "precedent" existed for such a practice. And, of course, that is the very essence of what we speak of today as biblical "commands" and "examples."

A Unique Statement of Faith

As much as being a tool of biblical interpretation and application, even more so is our hermeneutic a statement of faith in God's revelation to man and, therefore, in the importance of the written Word. Of faith in the integrity of the biblical writings themselves, and in the authority of Holy Scripture as the ultimate, infallible guide to our life with God. Of faith in the importance of apostolic pattern for the work and worship of the church, and in the richness of spiritual Truth for the one who seeks a spiritual God. In fact, it was respect for the Word that led godly men in search of a method by which to understand God's revelation.

That is how our fundamental approach to hermeneutics was viewed in 1809, and that is how it is honored even today (with the possible exception of those folks who have more of a love for doctrinal wrangling than humble submission to God's leading). More than simply a "hermeneutic," our formulation of "command, example, and necessary inference" is a rejection of human creeds and a commitment to the authority of God and his divine revelation.

Initially, a church creed is rarely viewed as a substitute for Scripture. Over time, however, more attention is typically paid to the creed than to Scripture itself. What allows this to happen is the fact that creeds crystalize a *particular interpretation* of Scripture. That is precisely where our hermeneutic is different. It commits us to the authoritative leading of Scripture without stating any doctrinal beliefs.

If "command, example, and necessary inference" is not nearly as grand as loftier statements of faith such as the Apostles' Creed, its very focus embodies a compelling rejection of *all* human creeds which formulate specific doctrinal beliefs, no matter how prosaic their language, no matter how biblical their content. Importantly, Acts 2:38 may indeed be *our scripture*, but "command, example, and necessary inference" has never become *our creed* as other fellowships envision a "creed." Quite to the contrary, our hermeneutic remains a graphic reminder that we have no written statement of doctrinal beliefs. (What *unwritten* creed we may have developed over time is another matter.) Despite its place of honor in our particular tradition, our hermeneutic has never become a substitute for Scripture. Indeed, how could it, when its very purpose is to call us back to the Word itself with all the force it can muster!

And therein lies its greatest appeal. To a religious community torn apart by denominational schism in the 18th and 19th centuries, the call of our restoration plea was a rally cry of freedom in Christ. It swept away human creeds, and opened the way for a fresh pursuit of Truth. Whereas (often with a tinge of embarrassment) we tend to see our hermeneutic as legalistic and narrow, the fact of the matter is that the essence of our approach to hermeneutics was born of a liberating spirit bent on opening previously closed doors.

If the statement "We speak where the Bible speaks and are silent where the Bible is silent" was the genius that captured the imagination of a strife-torn denominational world, it was the spirit of "command, example, and necessary inference" (even if not precisely articulated early on) that sought to turn that imagination into reality. Even if but few people knew (much less could spell) the word *hermeneutic*, they nevertheless had no doubt as to where it led. For a world weary of credal roadblocks, it meant getting "back to the Bible!" Back to basics. Back to "book, chapter, and verse!"

How many of us, then, owe our very faith to those who went before us, decrying human innovation and blowing the dust off of the Book of books which for too long had been ignored? How many people who've never given a second thought to "command, example, and necessary inference" have been led nevertheless by its silent tutoring to faith-filled lives in obedience to God's Word?

In Praise of Pattern

We tend to forget, of course, that our hermeneutic has both a *formal* name—"command, example, and necessary inference"—and a *nickname*: "Pattern." *Pattern* is the name we most often use when referring to our hermeneutic. It is the biblical *pattern* which we attempt to follow. It is the "pattern of sound teaching"[2] which we try to perpetuate in those who follow after us. Whereas the *formal* name itself is never found in Scripture, in both the Old and New Testaments, its *nickname* is a household word. It was this pattern of which Thomas Campbell spoke in the *Declaration and Address*: "The original pattern laid down in the New Testament; the divine Word is our standard; making a rule of it and it alone; what is expressly revealed and enjoined in the Holy Scriptures."

The first time we run across the word *pattern* in the Bible is when God is telling Moses exactly how he wants the tabernacle to be built.[3] In the midst of giving his many intricate instructions, God solemnly warns Moses, "Make this tabernacle and all its furnishings exactly like the pattern I will show you." The pattern to which God referred was so detailed that it included even the color of the curtain loops (blue) and the type of clasps (gold) that were to be used in the tabernacle's construction. We're not just talking here about broad architectural guidelines or some vaguely stated preference for gothic over neo-classical style of design. To God, even the most minute details of the pattern were important.

The reason for God's attention to detail is made clearer when we read Hebrews chapter eight. There, the writer speaks of Christ serving in the heavenly sanctuary, "the true tabernacle set up by the Lord, not by man."[4] Comparing our high priest, Christ, with the high priests of Israel, the writer continues: "They serve at a sanctuary that is a copy and shadow of what is in heaven. This is why Moses was warned when he was about to build the tabernacle: 'See to it that you make everything according to the pattern shown you on the mountain.'"[5]

Paul had used the same word—*pattern*—in writing to Timothy: "What you heard from me, keep as the pattern of sound teaching, with faith and love in Christ Jesus."[6] The pattern principle dovetailed nicely with Paul's observation just a few paragraphs later that "all Scripture is God-breathed and is useful for teaching, rebuking, correcting and training in righteousness, so that the man of God may be thoroughly equipped for every good work."[7]

Biblical patterns matter because they are *God's* patterns.

Why else would God have revealed himself to us except to set forth the way that works—the way that his *church* best functions, the way that *we* best function? As our Creator, surely he must know!

Constitution or Model?

That said, I am nevertheless sympathetic to the suggestion that New Testament patterns are more specifically directed to individual faith and righteousness than to the work and worship of the church. For instance, Paul uses *pattern* in this sense when telling the Christians in Philippi: "Join with others in following my example, brothers, and take note of those who live according to the pattern we gave you."[8] In this regard, certainly, we in the church are vulnerable to a charge that we have abused our hermeneutic by employing it almost exclusively in determining formal church doctrine rather than applying it to the daily perfection of a holy life in Christ. Or even that we have failed to apply it sufficiently in the search for God, Christ, and the Holy Spirit—something we *ought* to have done, without leaving the other concerns undone.

"Pattern" can mean constitution, charter, and blueprint, or—in a far more personal sense—it can mean example, model, and mentor. Typically, we have tended to think of our hermeneutic primarily as a *constitution* for deciding doctrinal issues or as a *blueprint* for church organization and structure. It is this concept of pattern, of course, for which "command, example, and necessary inference" is best suited.

By contrast, how often have we thought of our hermeneutic as a *model* for Christian living or as a *mentor* of personal righteousness? Our hermeneutic appears to let us down somewhat when applied to scriptures which pertain more directly to life and godliness. When we look for a model of holiness, we rightly look more to a *Person* than to a *passage.*

Yet one cannot help but remember that the pattern principle itself was first established in connection with a structure designed for congregational worship (the tabernacle) and, in the letter to the Hebrews, is invoked in teaching the doctrinal superiority of Christ's priesthood over any earthly priesthood. Abuse in one direction does not warrant abuse in another direction. If we have failed to see how apostolic pattern is important in developing ourselves spiritually, the remedy is not found in abandoning apostolic pattern specifically directed toward doctrine, church organization, and congregational worship. It is not *abandonment* that we need, but *balance.*

Whether it be a hermeneutic aimed at determining the proper work and worship of the church, or a hermeneutic meant for personal spiritual growth, the Scripture is our only guide for what we are and do as Christians. More importantly, it is only through the Scriptures (the revelation of God's mind to man) that we can come to know God, Christ, and the Holy Spirit. Without the Scriptures, how could we ever learn about Jesus, who is the pattern-like incarnation of the Father?

Having a shared hermeneutic for determining the corporate work and worship of the church may not be as crucial or as lofty as coming to know God in the first place, but it becomes important once we do know God. And, at that point, having a pattern for how we are to conduct our mutual worship together may be as significant as having a model for righteous living. After all, it is in that crowded crossroads known as "the church" that our individual attempts at righteousness are likely to put us on a collision course with others in pursuit of the same goal.

I sometimes wonder whether there is not some divine purpose behind the divisions of Scripture which we know as the "Gospels" and the "Epistles." In the Gospels, Jesus is presented as our sublime spiritual model and our supreme example of righteousness. Peter reminds us: "Christ suffered for you, leaving you an example, that you should follow in his steps."[9] And Paul echoes that sentiment when he says, "Follow my example, as I follow the example of Christ."[10]

As "the Word made flesh,"[11] Christ himself is the *incarnate hermeneutic.* As John says in the prologue to his Gospel, "No one has ever seen God, but God the [Only Begotten], who is at the Father's side, has made him known."[12] It is Jesus, therefore, who has "interpreted" God for us, and Jesus who helps us to apply to our own lives the lessons we learn through him about the holiness of God.

Naturally, the Gospels *as text* and Jesus' own teachings inevitably require interpretation. What, precisely, are we meant to learn from Jesus? For example, we don't automatically know if we're supposed to pray just as Jesus prayed ("Thy Kingdom come!") or live exactly as Jesus lived (both unmarried and without possessions). But the "living hermeneutic" brings us to God like no other written words can— including, ironically, the very words which tell us about him. Not all the written words in Scripture taken together tell us as much about God as does *the* Word, Jesus Christ!

In the Epistles, on the other hand, we are given apostolic teaching aimed not only at further proclaiming Christ and calling us to Christ-like righteousness, but directed also toward the corporate functioning of the church. It is in this latter mode that we have need of a guiding hermeneutic to help us sort out how we ought to function as a fellowship of believers some twenty centuries removed from the audience to whom the apostles first directed their teaching. If "command, example, and necessary inference" is somewhat less suited as a hermeneutic for biblical guidelines regarding personal righteousness, it takes on increased importance when utilized as a hermeneutic for the functioning church.

Suppose We Didn't Have the Old Hermeneutic

Sometimes it is good to approach a subject through the back door. Have you ever wondered, for instance, what the shape of our shared faith would be like if we did *not* have a hermeneutic such as "command, example, and necessary inference"? Is it just a coincidence, for example, that virtually all fellowships *without* our hermeneutic have their notions of baptism so clearly out of sync with our own understanding of biblical teaching on this central feature of Christian doctrine? Would you ever have guessed that a person would need a hermeneutic of *any* kind in order to appreciate the importance of what we take for granted to be the scriptural teaching on this act of Christian initiation?

Is it just possible that well-intentioned believers miss the significance of baptism because their eyes have not been trained to look for what comes so naturally to us: "command, example, and necessary inference"? When we read about Jesus directing the apostles to teach and baptize the nations,[13] our minds automatically think in terms of a biblical imperative or "command." When we see instance after instance in the book of Acts where the apostles baptized believers upon their confession of faith,[14] we naturally formulate a pattern of practice based on apostolic "example." And when we read in Paul's letter to the Galatians that we are all "sons" of God by faith, having clothed ourselves with Christ through baptism,[15] we hardly hesitate to make the "necessary inference" that baptism is therefore crucial to our relationship with God.

It all seems so natural to us that we are left to wonder about everyone else: "How could they possibly *miss* it?" Perhaps we have simply given too little credit to the hermeneutic that we either take for granted or are all too eager to trash.

In a recent meeting with the Independent Christian Churches, I was surprised to learn that the significance of baptism is becoming more and more controversial. Perhaps it should not have been so surprising. Although we come from the same restoration background, the Independent Christian Churches have not maintained strict adherence to our hermeneutical roots. They refer only generally to the New Testament as a "model." This less strict approach (they would say less *legalistic* approach) may well have resulted in significant differences in the role of women in the church and, of course, in the use of instrumental music. Some might argue that there are other, more historical and social reasons for our differences. Yet I doubt those factors alone would explain their current misgivings about baptism. That one issue alone may be the most interesting—and most telling—commentary on the importance of having a more carefully articulated hermeneutic as a safeguard against doctrinal slippage.

Where religious tradition can perpetuate unbiblical practices, a vigorously applied hermeneutic like "command, example, and necessary inference" forces us to keep asking the tough question: "Is it *tradition* or *biblical teaching* that we are following?" (Where it is *not* vigorously applied, but is merely paid lip-service, our hermeneutic itself can become the agent of perpetuated tradition. All praise, then, to the *intent* of our hermeneutic, and due caution where it is *abused.*)

Of course, there is a flip-side to consider. Given the focus of our hermeneutic on matters principally of church organization and function, have our notions of the Spirit, discipleship, and servanthood unduly suffered? The danger is that any single perspective risks being too narrow.

With What Alternative Are We Left?

There's yet another way to come through the back door, and that is to ask, "What, after all, are we supposed to do when we encounter specific biblical imperatives and apostolic examples?" Are we simply to ignore them? If first century commands and examples were intended only for those who lived during that generation, then by what guidelines do those of us who live in a much later generation propose to seek personal righteousness, let alone decide how we should function as a church?

Hardly anyone among us would suggest that we simply ignore specific biblical imperatives, but there are many today who seriously urge—particularly regarding apostolic example—that times have changed and, therefore, that what we do today should be more in keeping with contemporary culture. But if we weigh anchor on the New Testament pattern, how can we ever have any confidence that we are not far adrift from the course God intended us to keep?

Have we ever stopped to consider why God caused holy men of old to record, not just the life of Christ, but also the work and worship of the first generation of Christians? If the ultimate aim of apostolic instruction regarding the work and worship of the church is to bring us back to God, as more and more are urging, then it becomes all the more important that we follow the apostles' authoritative lead in that specific area of Christian practice. Proper church organization and function does not in itself get us "right" with God. But improper church organization and function (whether because of sterile tradition or unbiblical innovation) may indeed get us "wrong" with God.

Ours, But Not Ours Alone

Having said that "command, example, and necessary inference" is *our* hermeneutic, it should not be thought that no one else has ever had a similar hermeneutic. We are not the first "restorationists" to come on the scene. As others have recently pointed out regarding our roots, we have inherited a long legacy of restoration thinking from others who also sought, with all the fervor they could muster, to get back to the biblical pattern.

In her 1982 Oxford doctoral dissertation, entitled "London Calvinistic Baptists (1689-1727)," Dr. M. D. MacDonald reports, for example, that "Like most 17th century protestants, London Calvinistic Baptists believed the New Testament contained a clear model for the church which it was incumbent on true believers to duplicate."

If others haven't always used the exact formulation of "command, example, and necessary inference," they nevertheless have pointed in the same direction. Where we may be somewhat different from other back-to-the-Bible fellowships is in our persistent dedication to the pattern principle. To our credit, we've been more rigorous and consistent in following the model than most others. (Could it be because of the way in which we articulated our commitment to scriptural authority?)

The point is that there is no mystery about the origin of "command, example, and necessary inference." As we can see by looking even outside of our fellowship, once people of faith commit themselves to following God's lead, there is really no option but to view Scripture as a divinely-inspired model—including its specific precepts and precedents, and whatever other implications naturally flow from them.

Because Scripture is given to us in the form of historical illustrations and divine imperatives, we are left with no alternative but to follow their direction in our quest to know God. The particular method we happen to use to interpret and apply Scripture did not *just happen.* It was not made up out of thin air. We follow scriptural directives and precedent precisely because that is all we have to go on.

When push comes to shove, there are only a limited number of ways to interpret anything! In fact, whenever we want to understand someone, we generally look to two things: What a person *says* and what a person *does*. What could correspond more to our everyday, automatic, built-in hermeneutic than "commands" (sayings) and "examples" (doings)? When we instinctively look to precept and precedent, we're simply doing what comes naturally.

Some scholars for whom I have great respect insist that we must begin chronologically and theologically with God, Christ, and the Holy Spirit—not some hermeneutical formula. But that approach assumes the very conclusion we are trying to reach. How are we to know God, Christ, and the Holy Spirit except through divine revelation? And how are we to understand divine revelation without interpreting it? Before we can use God, Christ, and the Holy Spirit as our hermeneutic for such matters as the work and worship of the church, some other hermeneutic must first come into play. If we seek to proceed without *any* hermeneutic (conscious or unconscious), we can have *no* access to God's Word.

"Command, example, and necessary inference"—whatever its imperfections—is not the message-obscuring formula its critics want to make it into. It bears no resemblance to a human creed. It is not an addition to the Bible. It does not take precedence over Scripture. Nor was it ever intended to minimize the search for God, Christ, and the Holy Spirit.

More than anything else, "command, example, and necessary inference" points away from itself and away from *any* human formulation. Where is it pointing? To the Scriptures. *Why* to the Scriptures? To get us back to how we ought to live and worship as Christians. And *why* is that important? So that we can come to know God!

I assume we all would agree that anyone suggesting that we can know God without his revelation is treading on dangerous territory. But, given the very nature of that revelation, anyone suggesting that we can look at God's revelation without paying heed to its express directives and patterns for right living and worship is surely treading on the same dangerous territory. It's no good acknowledging the revelation itself if we refuse to acknowledge the specific avenues by which that revelation comes to us.

A Symbol of Allegiance

Whether we decide outright to ignore biblical imperatives or simply minimize the importance of apostolic example, we run a great risk of impudently affronting the God who has loved us enough to reveal himself to us and to steer us safely in paths of holiness. Our hermeneutic is simply another way of affirming our submission to his leading. It is our pledge of allegiance, as it were, to his divine sovereignty.

Perhaps some people are right to accuse us of doing too much flag-waving when it comes to honoring our particular hermeneutic. Perhaps they are right when they suggest that too often we have forgotten the commitment *for which it stands.* But just try burning the flag of "command, example, and necessary inference" and we will likely find ourselves confused about what we stand for as the people of God—a church with neither constitution nor character; a fellowship lacking the very spirit and holiness that so many today rightly seek.

FOUR

Book, Chapter, And *Verse*

"To rest upon a formula is a slumber that, prolonged, means death."
—Oliver Wendell Holmes

Given the respect I have expressed for "command, example, and necessary inference," it might be presumed that I have little sympathy with the call for a new hermeneutic. Yet I am not unsympathetic with the concerns being articulated by many among our fellowship who are conscientiously trying to move us toward a more dynamic spiritual relationship through the way that we understand Scripture.

For many years, long before I ever heard any talk of a new hermeneutic, I've questioned whether we have settled for "second-best" in our understanding of the Bible. Yet, I would suggest that our failure to fully appreciate the biblical text hasn't always, or even mostly, had to do with the so-called "old hermeneutic." In fact, I suggest that much of our present discontent could be better understood by close scrutiny of a number of seemingly-unrelated factors unwittingly working together to bring about a "restorationist" result never intended. As we think together about these various factors, I am acutely aware that my observations principally reflect my own experience in the church, which may be totally unlike your own. I am also aware of the tyranny of time and space which too easily can lead to overgeneralization. For every generality that might be stated, exceptions undoubtedly could be marshalled. But the nature of even positive criticism demands that we have some point of departure, even if it is not fully adequate to the task.

Finally, I should also say that this chapter deals with a retrospective which may no longer be representative of our fellowship. (On the other hand, some of us may see ourselves more than we want to.) Certainly "the cultural church" has already moved a far distance from past practices and perspectives, as witnessed by the very discussion in which we are involved. However, if what we are talking about is our roots, then—as others have recently pointed out—they are the very roots by which we have been shaped and from which we can never be totally extricated.

Institutionalizing the Church

As a starting point, it may be helpful to carefully examine our dominant perspective of the church as an institution. As I expressed in my book on baptism, I believe that we have tended to elevate the *church* of Christ over the *Christ* of the church. Looking back on the way we often packaged our presentation of the gospel, it was almost as if (despite what we said at the moment of immersion) we were baptized into the church instead of being baptized into Christ.

Becoming part of the body seemingly became the *object* of faith, rather than its *by-product*. At Pentecost, the church was for the already-saved, not the other way around. ("And the Lord added to their number daily those who were being saved."[1]) Our primary identification with the church is reflected, for example, in the way that we have referred to ourselves most often, not simply as Christians, but as "members of the church."

Our focus on the church was a well-intended effort to counter denominationalism with its many departures from biblical pattern, but we concentrated on such things as the organization, work, worship, and name of the church, rather than on the power of the gospel, the cross of Christ, and our individual relationships with God.

If our hermeneutic is related in some way to this particular focus, does it play the part of the chicken or the egg? Did our hermeneutic define our focus, or did our focus define our hermeneutic? As likely as not, our hermeneutic was forced into the limelight because of the goal we had already established, which was to counter denominationalism by restoring New Testament Christianity.

It should be noted, parenthetically, that "countering denominationalism" has been a bittersweet experience in our fellowship. The early restorationists were primarily intent upon reconstructing the New Testament church *as an alternative* to the denominational division of their time. Unfortunately, some later church leaders seemed to be bent on simply *beating up* denominations, perhaps to enhance their own personal reputations as "defenders of the faith." In their case, denomination-bashing became an end in itself. However, for the early restorationists, our counter-denominational focus was part of a bigger picture in which the "old hermeneutic" was useful to achieving the overall goal.

At least in the first instance, it was not the power of the gospel, the cross of Christ, or our individual relationship with God that separated us from denominational doctrines. Virtually the entire "Christian community" agreed on the basic teachings regarding Jesus of Nazareth.

The concerns we felt compelled to share with others involved biblical patterns about *responding* to the gospel and *appropriating* the cross of Christ in our worship and personal relationship with God. And how else were we going to call people closer to biblical guidelines but by appealing to the idea of "divine pattern"?

The problem is that we became the victims of our own success. In hoping to ensure *substance* through proper *form,* we succumbed to the ever-present temptation to elevate form over substance. Our concern gradually shifted from *spiritual* to *ritual.* And in that pursuit, our hermeneutic (standing bashfully at the back of the building) was only reluctantly dragged into the spotlight. Our hermeneutic was the "right man for the job," if only the job hadn't taken on a role out of all proportion to the basic gospel message.

What we are seeing today is a recognition by many that we are wobbling aimlessly as a fellowship because we have worried more about *method* than *message.* As journalists might put it, we've put the wrong "spin" on the facts. The problem is not the "facts" themselves, as some are suggesting, but the "spin" we put on them. When we read the Bible, are we looking primarily for *method* or *message*?

Of course, looking for either one to the exclusion of the other (the very thing that concerned us about denominationalism) always throws us out of balance. Ironically, where we sought to bring balance to others (by emphasizing the importance of method), we got ourselves out of balance by forgetting the centrality of the message.

It is not the *church* of Christ that we want to be, but the church *of Christ*. If that steadfastly remains our goal and aim, then, both corporately and individually, we will strive ever more earnestly to be the *people of Christ*—not simply "members of the church," or even merely "Christians" if all that means to us is "wearing the right name."

From Gospels to Epistles

Keeping in mind that our goal was to counter denominational *practices*, as opposed to denominational *faith*, we naturally invited our religious neighbors to a closer study of the Epistles, which concentrate more on church practice than do the Gospels. Without anyone willing it to be so, Paul's teaching took on a significance almost greater than Christ's. "The Sermon on the Mount" virtually took a back seat to Peter's sermon on Pentecost. We knew more of pattern than parable; more of rule than rationale.

We didn't overwork our hermeneutic in determining the pattern for church organization, worship, and identity as much as we simply came to deemphasize any part of the New Testament which didn't concern itself with those important doctrinal details. Unfortunately, what became deemphasized was at the very heart of the matter—the Gospels.

Sure, we *studied* the Gospels, and we *knew* the Gospels, but we didn't *major* in the Gospels. (Nor did we develop the hermeneutical tools which allowed us to dive as deeply into the Gospels as we had into Paul.) Given our non-denominational focus, we majored in the Epistles and minored in the Gospels.

This was true even in our approach to evangelism. And yet that, too, was probably merely a matter of circumstance.

Had we been teaching Hindus or Buddhists, we undoubtedly would have started off with the gospel accounts of the life and teachings of Christ. But those whom we were evangelizing were our Christ-accepting neighbors—Baptists, Methodists, Presbyterians, and Catholics.

They already knew about Christ and believed in him much the same as we did. From our perspective, it was not the death, burial, and resurrection that they needed to hear, but the believer's response to the gospel as outlined in apostolic teaching (the Epistles) and in the examples of first-century Christians (the book of Acts). No wonder, then, that we had so many Bible classes devoted to Acts and the Epistles. They provided the very ammunition we needed for our assault on denominationalism.

To the extent that our focus may have become a fault, in fairness it should at least be stated that the central message of the gospel always loomed large in the background. It's just that it wasn't always center stage. Had you asked anyone what was more important—method or message, Epistles or Gospels, church or Christ—you would always have gotten the right answer. The gospel message of Christ was always at the core of our faith and doctrine. Always. The problem was that we came off preaching, teaching, talking, and writing more about proper methods of the functioning church as derived from the Epistles.

Topical Versus Expository

Even in our closer scrutiny of the Epistles, we had the option of giving a more "gospel-like" spin to the apostolic letters. Skim back through Romans, the Corinthian letters, Ephesians, and Colossians, and you'll see that Paul structures his letters so as to move from Christ to the church, from rationale to rule, from message to method. For Paul, it's always a "since-then" approach. "Since" we know this about Christ, "then" we should live in a particular way, or worship together as a church in some specific manner.

But once again, given our stated goal to counter denominationalism through restoring New Testament Christianity, we rarely chose that option. We hurried from what we presumed to be common ground (the cross of Christ), to the rules and regulations governing the work and worship of the church—ignorance of which had caused the lamentable sectarian division among believers in Christ. In doing so, however, we were unwittingly led to a *topical* approach to Scripture.

Somewhat oversimplified, here is how the topical approach works. If our concern is the proper *name* for the church, for example, we dredge through Acts and the Epistles looking for the proper designation. If the subject changes and we're talking with our neighbors about *how one becomes a Christian*, again we go through the same dredging process. And on it goes, topic after topic, until we have lifted supporting passages from Acts and the Epistles answering all of our questions from what appears to be the first-century pattern.

Often left behind in our earnest search for biblical guidelines was the balance between Christ and church, message and method, rationale and rule. Worse yet, we always ran the risk of abusing context. Topical sermons and Bible class lessons led to scripture-seeking scavenger hunts in which individual verses—sometimes as many as twenty or thirty per sermon—were grabbed from the text, organized by outline, and presented as the whole of God's truth on the matter. (And what could have been more of a boon to this approach than the chart and the now-obligatory overhead projector!)

By contrast, expository sermons, which take clusters of verses in context and draw out (or *expose*) their core message, were not as suitable for the goal at hand. If what you wanted to address was a given *topic* of importance, the careful exposition of only one passage might well overlook what other passages contribute to the discussion.

"Proof-texting" is another similar process, used principally in our formal and informal debates with others. In proof-texting, specific biblical texts are not regarded holistically, as integral parts of larger documents having broad scope and intent, but narrowly, as argumentative proof for some point of doctrine. "This is what the Bible teaches about that, and here are the dozen passages which prove it."

Proof-texting need not be a bad thing. One gets the idea that Paul must have done a bit of good old-fashioned proof-texting in the synagogue, "For he vigorously refuted the Jews in public debate, proving from the Scriptures that Jesus was the Christ."[2] But if our own proof-texting often enlisted various passages in aid of a worthy cause, it sometimes left them wounded and bleeding from having been pressed into action beyond their original marching orders.

Taken together, proof-texting and the topical approach had their own interesting spinoff. Even our style of preaching became somewhat unique. Traditionally, sermons in our fellowship have been more topical, multi-versed, and doctrine-driven than expository, text-based, and message-driven.

Just One of Many Wide-Ranging Results

What a critical first step we had taken, then, in determining that our primary goal was to counter denominationalism. That one historically-based decision had determined not only our predominant use of a given hermeneutic, but also our focus on the church as an institution, our emphasis on Acts and the Epistles, and even our mostly-topical sermon style!

Yet even that was not the full extent of its impact. All those factors, when combined together, gave us a unique identity as a fellowship that soon became almost as important to us as the worthy goal we were committed to achieve. In trying so desperately to combat the evils of denominationalism, we ourselves became caught in its web.

Among other examples that might be noted, simply consider how what started out as a clearly biblical designation, "church of Christ," ended up becoming a more denominational-sounding "Church-of-Christ" church! Readily acknowledging that the scriptural pattern also speaks of the body of the saved as "the Way"[3] and "the church of God,"[4] we have selectively chosen a capital "C" Church of Christ as the most biblical (*only* biblical?) designation for the church.

Such denominational-like usage crops up almost everywhere you turn. I continue to be amazed, for example, when I sit among a group of preachers and elders as they introduce themselves around the room. "I am Joe Bloggs from the Anytown *Church of Christ*," says first one, then another. Why not simply, "I am Joe Bloggs from the Anytown *church*?" Not content to be simply Christ's church (or one of the local congregations thereof), we cling ever so closely to our unique "Church of Christ" identity.

I recognize that what I am saying here is supremely sensitive, going to the very name by which we are identified. But it may be one of the best examples of where we've made some wrong turns, and how we've missed the real import of the Scriptures which we wish to honor. In this case, "What's in a name?" may provide an explanation for the identity crisis we seem to be going through.

What's disturbing initially is a kind of self-validating use of the name "Church of Christ." If we are the "Church of Christ" in *name*, so we seem to think, then surely we must be the church of Christ in *fact*. Naturally, calling ourselves "Church of Christ" doesn't automatically make us Christ's church any more than placing a Cadillac insignia on the hood of a Ford makes the Ford a Cadillac. Put another way—if in fact we *are* the church of Christ, it doesn't come from any label that we might wear, even if we can find the exact same words used in the New Testament.

What I am getting at is more than a quibble about the church's name. In the strictest sense, the church has *no name*. It is simply the church *belonging to Christ*—the called-out "church of God in Corinth," and the called-out "church of God" in Abilene, Nashville, Vienna, and Oxford. It is the body of Christ in the United States, the body of Christ in England, and the body of Christ in China.

Looking for a scriptural name seemed necessary in countering the obvious denominational error of attaching human names to Christ's church. Yet, we got so caught up in the castigation of "wrong names" that we ended up finding a "right name" where none really was to be found. And that brought us trouble in two different ways.

First of all, we simply over-formalized Paul's closing salutation to the Romans: "All the churches of Christ send greetings."[5] Suppose Paul had said (as he well could have), "All the churches of *God* send greetings." Would our signs and ads in the Yellow Pages now read "Church of God"?

What we've done in taking a description of the church (the church that belongs to Christ) and formalizing it into a title for the church is similar to the evolution of family names. "John's son" eventually became "Johnson;" and the "son of William" became "Williamson." What we've done is to take the "church of Christ," added a capital "C", and turned it into a formal name it was never intended to be.

Far more serious is the fact that, in order to bolster our formalization of "Church of Christ," we went so far as to distort the use of the word *name* in other contexts. Consider, for example, Colossians 3:17, cited on the rare occasion in support of the church's authorized name: "And whatever you do, whether in word or deed, do it all in the name of the Lord Jesus...." Nothing in the context suggests that Paul is talking about a name for the church. The word *name* in this context more appropriately refers to the kingship and authority of Jesus. And this leads us to yet another good illustration.

Even the closing tag with which we end our prayers—"In Jesus' name, Amen"—reflects a formalization never intended. The text says, "*Whatever you do....*" Are we understanding the correct meaning of the passage when we insist on the formal repetition of those words in connection only with prayer? Praying "in Jesus' name" is perfectly consistent with the passage. But Paul's point has more to do with the spirit with which we lead our lives before the sovereign Lord: nothing without his leading; nothing without his lordship.

Becoming Too Well-*Versed*

Stay with me on this one. I'm not suggesting that we quit offering our prayers "in Jesus' name" or disfellowship anyone who does or does not put a capital "C" on "church of Christ." I'm headed in a different direction altogether. My concern here is our traditional method of studying the Bible.

Our topical approach has led us toward what, to all appearances, looked like a commendable "book, chapter, and verse." More often than not, however, the reality was that it led us to a collection of *single verses*, taken out of the context of chapter and book. One verse here; another there.

Perhaps you've heard it said: "It only takes one verse to establish biblical authority." Of course, that is true—assuming that the "one verse" is not twisted from its proper context and was originally intended to be directive of our own response to God. Sadly, our record in the use of individual verses has not always been exemplary.

It bears noting that the danger of individual verses is not found exclusively in the sporadic search for guidelines under a topical approach to the Bible. Another way in which we have placed an undue burden on individual verses is found in the traditional Bible class. If Bible study books tended to take a topical approach, the alternative of text-based classes was not altogether free of problems.

Your own experience may vary, but I grew up on a steady diet of "verse-by-verse" studies. One verse would be read (even if it was an incomplete thought or partial sentence) and then comments made on it. Slowly and deliberately, verse by tedious verse, the class would plod its way through each chapter.

One might think that such an approach to Bible study would be commendable and lead naturally to a more contextual and expository study. Yet, too many times no attempt was made to get an overview of the entire epistle or to see how the "one verse" fit into the context of even the immediate paragraph. And you simply wouldn't believe the kinds of conclusions that could be reached in the process!

Any outsider observing our verse-by-verse studies might assume that the Bible, as originally written, was divided into chapters and verses. (Unfortunately, both the earlier King James Version and the contemporary New American Standard Version present each verse as its own paragraph, reinforcing that misconception.) But chapters and verses are only a relatively recent feature of the printed Word (verses, as late as the 16th century), and may, in this regard at least, be more harmful than helpful.

The verse divisions, in particular, are completely arbitrary. In fact, sometimes they are sufficiently whimsical that one wonders whether it was really a good idea for Robert Stephanus (or Stephens) to have been riding his horse between Paris and Lyons while doing his work. The way some verses end, you can almost tell where the horse hit a rut in the road!

For whatever other value they may have been in terms of memorization or ease of location, the simple fact is that verses have robbed us of context. They have oftentimes captured our *divided* attention when what they needed was our *undivided* attention!

It would be interesting to know the present extent to which this verse-by-verse approach is still used in the church today. One suspects that it is a dying feature of our fellowship. (Mind you, the non-biblical philosophical discussions which have taken its place can make one yearn for the good old days of verse-by-verse!) Yet, however limited this time-honored style of teaching may be today, there can be no doubt but that we have inherited more than a generation of its results.

Incidentally, if one thinks that undue emphasis on individual verses is to be associated only with the church's "legalistic, rationalistic" past, the evidence is to the contrary. One remarkable irony of our current struggle over the role of women is the widespread practice of extracting (wholly out of context) the single verse of Galatians 3:28 in a disingenuous attempt to use "neither male nor female" to overcome the many specific instructions which unquestionably call for male spiritual leadership.

As any objective reading will indicate, Paul's letter to the Galatians is all about our vertical relationship with God—not our horizontal relationships with each other. In Christ, says Paul, all racial, social, and gender barriers fall *with regard to salvation.* It was not Paul's purpose to discuss the issues of special gender responsibilities which he specifically addresses in his later letters. Today's misuse of Galatians 3:28 is a monument to our irrepressible temptation to read into Scripture what we want it to say, rather than having the humility to hear what it actually says.

Hoping that we might be able to get a better handle on context, I've tried in a small way to do something about it. If you've seen a copy of *The Narrated Bible* (or *The Daily Bible*), you may have noticed that all chapter and verse designations have been placed in the margin rather than in the text itself. At the risk of also being second-guessed (though I assure you I rode no horses), I have re-paragraphed the Scriptures according to natural thought flow, and hopefully pointed the reader, not just to text, but to context.

It might also be worth noting that Alexander Campbell did much the same with his "immersion version." Ignoring traditional chapter and verse divisions, he organized the text by what he called "sense paragraphs." His having done that takes on added significance in the current climate of criticism of his supposed bent toward a rationalistic, topic-oriented, and verse-exalting scientific method. The fact is that our earliest restoration roots reflect a high respect for biblical context. If we've lost that respect along the way, it is not Campbell's fault.

"Book, chapter, and verse" is the right idea. But as a fellowship, we may have been shaped as much by the *verse* as by the *book*. The risk is that if we live by the verse, we can also die by the verse.

New Needs, New Goals, New Focus

For all their potential abuse, topical sermons and verse-by-verse studies need not be our enemy. Nor need we fear the use of selective passages which point to religious error. What we must avoid at all cost is the unfair manipulation of God's Word under the guise of appealing to biblical authority. For even if we could survive our own mishandling of Scripture, we could never hope to reach out to a world already skeptical of imposed authority in any form. And, as we have already seen, that world is rapidly changing.

Realizing that in the past our approach to Scripture has been molded by our attempt to counter denominationalism, one can understand some of the motivation behind the current movement for change within our fellowship. Our neighbors are no longer the "churched," but the "unchurched." Unlike times past, there is not necessarily any common ground of faith in Christ. For the postmodern, New Age, secular generation (which we will describe further in the next chapter), any effort aimed almost exclusively at correcting church doctrine is likely to be misplaced zeal. In reaching out to others, it's the basic *message* we must concentrate on for the moment. It's the *cross* that we must hold up before a post-Christian world, both in Scripture and in our lives.

If, by the grace of God, the shame of the cross ever breaks through the arrogance of our age, then hopefully there will be time enough and openness enough for teaching about method, doctrine, and detail. Our only concern at that point will be whether *we ourselves* any longer care about the details—or whether, like the denominationalists before us, we have concentrated so much on the "since" (of core faith in Christ) that we have forgotten all about the "then" (of how God has asked us to respond as a body of believers).

FIVE

Changing Times, Changing Issues

*Theological preaching is deservedly unpopular if all it does
is settle a lot of problems people never heard of, and ask a lot
of questions nobody ever asks....*
—Robert J. McCracken: *The Making of the Sermon*

On the front page of a recent Sunday edition, the *Los
Angeles Times* carried the following news items: "Gay-Rights
Bill Veto Draws Angry Reaction"; "Washington State Voters
May Grant the Right to Die"; and "Abortion Protestors Jailed
for Picketing Clinic." Other headlines read: "Surrogate
Mother Sues Couple for Custody of Child"; "Fetal Harvesting
for Alzheimer's Disease"; and "Think-Tank Calls for Legaliza-
tion of Drugs."

Abortion, euthanasia, drugs, homosexual rights, fetal
experimentation, and surrogacy are only a few of the dra-
matic social issues which vie for attention at the dawn of the
21st century. Divorce is still taking its devastating toll, along
with homelessness, dysfunctional families, and teenage sui-
cides which continue to escalate to shocking levels. In inner
cities and suburbs alike, crime continues to inundate every
strata of society. Gang violence threatens to destroy the very
core of American decency, and pornography has become
commonplace even on major network television. And what
more graphic reminder do we need of society's thin moral
veneer than the riots and looting which brought Los Angeles
to its knees?

In a larger context, the world is no longer made up simply of nation-states, but is moving toward a "new world order." The goal is a global community in which there will be commonly-shared political—perhaps even spiritual—values. Who knows what Christian values will be compromised along the way?

Telecommunication has shrunk the world to the point where wars are no longer fought only along distant battle fronts, but on 24-hour news channels right in our own living rooms. If Christian evangelism is thankfully going over the airways to lands we've never before been able to reach, other ideologies and religious beliefs are being beamed back our way in return.

Islam, for example, is no longer a mysterious Middle-East religion that constitutes just another chapter in a world religions textbook. If Islam tends to be equated with terrorism, hostage crises, and higher prices at the gas pump, it has also become one of the fastest-growing religions on the face of the globe, spurred on by the evangelistic fervor of Muslim fundamentalism.

On the home front, the New Age Movement has emerged from a fringe cult belief system of the "drug-culture 60's" and the "Shirley MacLaine 80's" to become mainstream thinking for a growing number of people in government, business, and education. Reincarnation and a fascination for the paranormal are only window dressing for a spiritualized quest for personal power in which we are all a part of the infinite Oneness of the universe and of divinity itself. The message of the New Age is nothing short of the shocking affirmation: You and I are God!

In the New Age, spiritual redefinitions abound. *God* is now *God Force* (as in "May the Force be with you"). *Soul* and *spirit* (even the *Holy Spirit*) are now *energy*. *Atonement* (as in Jesus' sacrificial death) is now *at-one-ment*, which is said to come with the realization that you and I are God. *Christ* has become *Christ-consciousness*, something all of us can have when we connect with our "Higher Selves."

Along the way, Christ and Buddha have been put on the same spiritual plane, and all religions have become interchangeable. Hinduism? Buddhism? Christianity? Pick and choose as you wish. The message of our times is that all religions lead to the same end, having in common the great principles of peace, love, and happiness.

Different Questions For Different Times

Who could have guessed how far we would come from the days when we had the luxury of worrying only about the doctrinal correctness of infant baptism, instrumental music, kitchens in the church building, and whether women ought to wear hats during worship? Gone are the days when moral issues could easily be reduced to dancing, smoking, drinking, and "mixed bathing."

When again will we see a time where abortion is not an option for pregnancy outside of wedlock, or ceases to be the standard medical procedure when a prenatal test indicates the fetus has Down's syndrome? How can we ever turn the clock back to the age of innocence when divorce and even alcoholism were hardly visible in the Lord's church? The times, they are indeed a-changing!

If "command, example, and necessary inference" can help us know something of baptism and instrumental music, what can it tell us about the morality of parental surrogacy or artificial insemination? If our hermeneutic is instructive regarding the frequency with which we ought to take the Lord's Supper or the proper qualifications for elders, how does it help us convert our New Age neighbors from their belief in extraterrestrials, out-of-body experiences, and "channeled" spirit guides?

Does "command, example, and necessary inference" come to our aid in any direct way when we are trying to convince a Muslim that Jesus is superior to Mohammed? Can we fall back on our hermeneutic when someone asks what we think about *in vitro* fertilization? Or whether street drugs ought to be legalized, or how Christians ought to feel about environmental issues or perhaps animal rights?

Our dialogues are no longer the fierce doctrinal debates we used to have with our Baptist friends about whether we are saved before being baptized. Or with our Catholic neighbors, regarding their veneration of Mary. Or with the Mormons or the Jehovah's Witnesses who knock on our door two by two. No longer do we have even the luxury of in-fighting among ourselves over the proper organization of the church, or church-run orphans' homes, or church-related colleges. Who knows? Are we even able to afford the luxury of battling over whether there ought to be a "new hermeneutic"?

Today's issues and questions are on a grander, or perhaps more intensely personal scale than ever before. We're talking to altogether different kinds of people now about a host of things to which the Bible makes no direct reference, whether by way of a "command" or an "example." And even if there are *inferences* which indirectly may be drawn to help answer the challenging questions of our "brave new world," the inferences often seem far more remote than the qualifying adjective "necessary" would imply.

Don't Write Off Our Hermeneutic Yet

With all these dizzying issues and questions swirling around the modern Christian, it would be easy to write off any discussion of hermeneutics as archaic and irrelevant. Some may ask, "Does God really want us to spend time discussing whether we can use instruments in worship when there are 1.5 million unborn children being killed in America each year through legalized abortion?" And it is a *very* good question!

Whatever else we may say about it, the time has come for those of us who are Christians to look around us and wake up to our society's shocking moral standards. God doesn't call us solely to be keepers of the Kingdom within the comfortable confines of the church. He calls us, as the prophets of old urged time and again, to protect the weak and vulnerable and to work for justice.

Yet we must not give up on our hermeneutic simply because it may be suited to answering some questions better than others. Would we throw away a hammer simply because we've now discovered there are some screws needing attention rather than nails? Of course not. When there are nails to be driven in, we'll still need a hammer. Likewise, whenever we look to the work and worship of the church, we must have some way of determining from Scripture how God wants us to proceed.

If there are questions today which neither Jesus nor the apostles directly addressed, the answers to those questions which they *did* directly address are as valid in principle for us today as they were for Christians in the first century. We needn't throw out yesterday's hermeneutic baby with tomorrow's brave-new-world bath water. Simply because we may have no specific pattern regarding certain matters gives us no license to ignore divine mandate in other areas where we have clear biblical teaching.

Shifting Our Focus

One thing we may have to do in response to a more complex set of moral questions is to shift our focus away from matters merely pertaining to the work and worship of the church. In our comfortable pew, we are very, very far from the world around us. In many ways, we're further away than we've ever been before.

The world around us today is not interested in what rituals of worship may or may not be authorized by Scripture. Most modern Americans have no intention of worshipping God, either one way or another. Nor do they perceive any need for a Savior, because, with every advance in moral relativism, they experience less and less moral guilt. Many (if not most) do not even understand that they have a *soul* which is accountable to God. If they have no *soul* and commit no *sin*, what need do they have of a *Savior*? When they don't even pretend to believe in the Bible, how impressed are they going to be if we attempt to appeal to them through "command, example, and necessary inference" as found in Holy Writ?

In some ways, we find ourselves in the same position as the apostle Paul. When he was in Jerusalem, he appealed to his Jewish hearers through the Scriptures, which they both knew and took to be authoritative[1] (even if they had effectively nullified them through human tradition). But when Paul was with the Greek philosophers on Mars Hill in Athens, he appealed, not to Scripture, but to universally knowable eternal truths, "as some of your own poets have said."[2] Where biblical commands and examples might have won the day with sincere Jews in Jerusalem, there was not a chance that people unfamiliar with Scripture would be convinced immediately by any kind of systematic method of interpreting God's Word.

Paul took his listeners as he found them. Step One for ancient pagans (as it must also be for modern American pagans) was to teach them about "AN UNKNOWN GOD." To a world brainwashed with the Darwinian notion of amoeba-to-man evolution, we must follow Paul's lead in affirming:

> The God who made the world and everything in it is the Lord of heaven and earth and does not live in temples built by hands. And he is not served by human hands, as if he needed anything, because he himself gives all men life and breath and everything else. From one man he made every nation of men, that they should inhabit the whole earth; and he determined the times set for them and the exact places where they should live.

Significantly, Paul made no reference to the book of Genesis in making this affirmation. Coming from their pagan perspective, the Greeks would not have given the slightest credence to "book, chapter, and verse." So Paul's initial appeal had to be to their natural senses through a universe which declares its Maker's praise. In proclaiming an eternal spiritual God from whom all material Creation proceeded, Paul radically overturned their pagan belief that the gods of the spirit world came from eternally existent nature.

How he must have captured their attention with the revolutionary idea that the material world came from Spirit, rather than vice versa! No wonder they had been worshipping gods who represented a material world. It was the material realm which they thought to be eternal and the material realm which they saw as the very essence of life.

Where neither "example" nor "inference" of *Scripture* could ever have served to convince them, Paul employed a *natural hermeneutic* using "example" and "inference." "Look around you," Paul said in effect. "Nature itself is your example leading you to God." Could Nature itself just have *happened*? Could we or anything else in this world have created what we observe? As you look about you at the vastness, orderliness, and harmony of nature, what "necessary inference" comes to your mind? Is it not the existence of an omnipotent God of Creation?

The point is that, in an age when biblical illiteracy abounds, and when the authority of Scripture is questioned even by those familiar with it, we are forced to reconsider our focus. We are no longer dealing simply with the Baptist mind, or the Catholic mind, but with pagan minds. *When, where,* and *how* we apply our hermeneutic must be more selective, more thoughtful, and more appropriate than ever before.

In a recent book on the subject of abortion addressed to a secular audience, I dared not appeal to the authority or pattern of Scripture. Not only would it have been ineffective, it would have been counterproductive. Throwing scriptures at secular readers would have confirmed their worst suspicions that I was just another "religious fanatic" whose arguments could be dismissed on that basis alone.

What they didn't know was that I was appealing to them through the truth of Scripture, but without quoting "book, chapter, and verse." More than that, like Paul in Athens I put that truth into the mouths of their "own poets." Or rather, I took that truth right *out of* the mouths of their own poets— namely, from that noted theologian, Woody Allen! His film, "Crimes and Misdemeanors," made many of the statements that I wanted to make but with more force and credibility than I could ever have commanded.

The sad irony in these changing times is that scriptural truths may have to be extracted from Scripture and paraphrased in order to be believed. Only when we have brought people to want to know God will we be able to point them to the Bible, and then to "book, chapter, and verse."

Time to Abandon Ship?

When we think about the mission of the church in a changing world, we could be excused for thinking that our old hermeneutic is, if not outdated, of only limited usefulness. Yet I suggest that we must reach just the opposite conclusion. Now more than ever we need to appreciate how critically our use of Scripture will determine whether we ever make an impact on a world to whom Scripture has become alien.

For starters, if the world sees that *we* can comfortably abandon the authority of Scripture when there are bits that we don't particularly like, then we have just given *them* the green light to ignore Scripture as well, whether in part or in whole. But it goes far deeper than mere perception and public relations. How we view and apply Scripture can actually make a dynamic difference to our culture in the New Age.

It can make a difference, first of all, by keeping *us* from succumbing to pagan thought and practice. We must not fool ourselves into thinking that we are immune. From within our own fellowship today, I can cite references being made to God as *the Force* and to the Holy Spirit as *energy*. Without intending any New Age implications, one well-respected author within the church has nevertheless dangerously said of God: "We are not neighbors to Jehovah...we are one with Him." And more dangerous yet: "We are co-God!" One can only hope that disclaimers which followed these statements in his book have been successful in steering the unwary away from the abyss of New Age thinking otherwise introduced.

My jaw fairly dropped when another widely-recognized personality in our fellowship publicly bemoaned the fact that he wishes he could believe in reincarnation, but—sadly—can't find it taught in the Bible! Have I missed something? Is there some reason why we would *want* to come back into a world of sin and suffering when, by God's grace, we can enjoy the eternal fellowship of heaven? Unfortunately, it doesn't end there. This same church leader recently began a prayer, saying, "God, we don't know how to address you—whether as *Father* God, *Mother* God...." What can I say!

Admittedly, making a connection between the New Age movement and pleas for a new hermeneutic may be a bit of a stretch for some. Yet, of one thing we can be sure. Whereas some people might contend that following the "old paths" has led us into various dead-end doctrinal ruts, we can be confident that our hermeneutic (when thoughtfully applied) will never allow us to fall into the tantalizing trap of New Age thinking or into any other form of obviously non-Christian heresy. If it does nothing else, a proper hermeneutic serves as a flashing caution light, warning us to slow down and carefully look both ways whenever current culture intersects with biblical instruction.

Old Paths for Modern Issues

The second way in which our understanding of Scripture can actually make a dynamic difference to our culture is in preempting the luxury of responding after-the-fact to current social and moral issues. If we as a society acknowledged (and actually practiced) clear biblical teaching on such matters as marriage and divorce, or God-given role relationships between men and women, you can rest assured that many of the social issues tearing our nation apart would be history.

Abortion, euthanasia, drugs, juvenile delinquency, homosexual rights, fetal experimentation, and surrogacy don't exist in a vacuum. Somewhere back down the line, they are all spin-offs from more basic biblical concerns. Abortion, for example, is not just about killing unwanted children, but about sexual morality, the spiritual value of human life, and woman's unique responsibility in the home. Abandon ship on any one of these more fundamental issues, and you'll soon find that the womb has become a tomb.

Likewise, make a dent in the principle of male spiritual leadership, and you'll soon discover young men growing up in dysfunctional families where the absence of strong male influence can lead to criminal delinquency and even ambivalence about one's sexual identity. It's no use wringing our hands over such radical political issues as gay rights if we are not prepared to reexamine how we might be contributing to the problem by ill-conceived hermeneutical approaches to seemingly unrelated biblical teaching.

In that same vein, you can forget about the recent headlines referring to "Race Riots in L.A." It wasn't primarily a racial issue or even a matter of economics. (Asian minorities came into this country with little more than the shirts on their backs and have managed to climb the ladder of success.) With blacks, there's much more of a root cause involved. When slavery forcibly removed fathers from the home, it brought about a matriarchal system that survives to this day. God bless the thousands of godly black women who have struggled single-handedly to raise their children, but what real chance have they had with a history of absentee husbands? In far too many cases, there has been no man around the house for young black men to model themselves after, and no one to *lay down the law.*

Lawlessness doesn't come from poverty; it comes from growing up without respect for authority. Male spiritual leadership is not abstract biblical theology or backward-thinking church doctrine. It's as practical as burning and looting are destructive. And lest we think we've seen the end of public disorder, consider this chilling thought: What slavery did involuntarily to black families, voluntary divorce is doing to white families. White families even in the church!

Hermeneutics, biblical authority, and church doctrine are more important to our society today than ever before. It's not about who can pass communion trays or lead a prayer. It's about God's order, social structure, and right-eousness exalting a nation![3]

Ideas have consequences. So do the specific methods of understanding Scripture which tend to shape our ideas. The Bible does not always directly address the issues of our time, but it always addresses the roots of any issue, if only we are willing to go back to the future. Hermeneutics is the time machine which takes us back to basics so that we can confidently launch out into the future of the church and confront whatever the latest social or moral issue might be. A hermeneutic which *wallows* in the past is rootbound and useless. But a hermeneutic which *snubs* the past jeopar-dizes the future.

If "command, example, and necessary inference" seems unrelated to the challenges of our "brave new world," then we have understood it too narrowly. The pattern of the New Testament was not designed solely for determining "church kinds of questions," but for producing Christian character. "Churchy things" are meant to have (and *do* have) a direct link to "character things."

Blue curtains and gold loops in the tabernacle were not part of some abstract exercise in following construction plans. Such details spoke to such weightier matters as God's divine majesty, man's strict obedience, and the correct prioritizing of material resources. It is likely that God cared little about the color blue. But he undoubtedly cared a great deal about how his people colored their character through obedience to his specific instructions.

There is no issue in any age about which God has remained silent. Somewhere in Scripture—look for it—God has spoken! And the chances are good that his words come to us in the form of some "command," some "example," or perhaps some "inference" which we can draw from more direct biblical instruction—even if it's sometimes found in such unlikely places as the many regulations regarding church organization and function.

This is the most crucial question: Are we willing to trust that, somewhere down the dusty roads of first century Judea, God has led us in paths of right living, even for a global community headed into the 21st century?

Part Two

THE RISK OF BECOMING A CULTURE-CAPTIVE CHURCH

Is There More to the Call for a New
Hermeneutic Than We Realize?

*That we should practice what we preach is
generally admitted; but anyone who preaches
what he and his hearers practice must incur the
gravest moral disapprobation.*
– Logan Pearsall Smith

SIX

"New Hermeneutic"— A Ship Without Anchor?

The church which is married to the Spirit of its Age will be a widow in the next.
— William Ralph Inge

The students in my Law and Morality seminar are blowing my mind! Most of them are culturalists to the core—and the party line they are parroting is just plain scary! In the opening session, I always ask the obvious question: "What is morality?" A lively hour of discussion ranges everywhere from utilitarian practicality (What works?), to majority rule (What do most people accept?), to power politics (Who has the sheer strength to impose their will on everyone else?).

"But is there no higher law, no natural law, no transcendent morality?" I prod. "No," comes the answer from these future guardians of law and order. "Is there nothing that could be described as absolute truth—no universal, absolute standards of right and wrong?" I ask hopefully? Again comes the resounding (and delightfully ironic) answer, "*Absolutely not!*"

I press on. "How about the question of evil? Is there such a thing as inherent evil?" Again the answer is "No." (In a generation of moral relativism, what other answer should I expect?)

It's then that I bring out my trump card. "Was not the Holocaust inherently evil?" I ask smugly, knowing full well that I've got them locked into an untenable position. After all, everybody and his cat knows that the Holocaust was inherently evil! But to my utter surprise, one student after another shakes his head "No." "The Holocaust was *not* inherently evil!"

Are they putting me on? No, they're serious—dead serious. And that's not the worst of it. In each of the last two years, even my *Jewish* students have agreed! If maybe—just *maybe*—you could understand non-Jews being conned into such nonsense, who ever would guess that Jewish students would join them in taking such an outrageous position?

This year, in my dumbfoundedness, I pressed one Jewish co-ed for a further explanation. "How can you possibly believe that the Holocaust was not inherently evil? Are you not totally outraged by it?" "Oh, sure," she said, "I'm personally offended by the thought of any wholesale slaughter of Jews, and I sure wouldn't want it happening to me or my family, but [hang on, here comes the all-important punch line] *I simply can't impose my morality on anyone else!"*

For our generation, tolerance has become the highest virtue. (Tolerance, that is, for everything and everyone other than those who would insist on absolute moral standards.) But, again, that should not come as a surprise from a culture which extols relativism and blurs all distinction between right and wrong. If there is nothing that is either inherently good or inherently bad, then we must accept everything as equally valid. If nothing is "right" and nothing is "wrong," then tolerance is our only option.

In addition to the matter of undiscriminating tolerance, it is important to point out that today's students have bought off on a "new morality" that is rudderless. There was a time— call it the "forties" and "fifties"—when everyone knew what was right and wrong. Even if we didn't always do what was right, we were willing to acknowledge that it was wrong. Then came the "sexual revolution sixties" when society's ideas about what was right and what was wrong dramatically changed. Even into the "seventies," it continued to be a time of unstoppable moral decline.

However, morality for today's generation is radically different—not simply by degree, but in kind. In the "new morality," there is no "right" and there is no "wrong." The "new morality" is nothing short of moral chaos, reminiscent of the period of Israel's judges in which "everyone did as he saw fit."[1]

Political Correctness Demands a New Hermeneutic

In the event you have not already heard about it, there is a nation-wide frenzy on college campuses to insure what is known as "political correctness" (often abbreviated simply as P.C.). "Political correctness" is nothing more than a benign catchphrase for "the liberal agenda." In other words, you and I have to tow the liberal line on issues like abortion, gay rights, and radical feminism, or else be reported to the sensitivity police for being intolerant.

The idea, of course, is to protect and promote minority rights—or at least what are *seen to be* minority rights. It seems that every vocal group of advocates today—regardless of the morality of their cause—must be accorded minority status, with all the respect that entails. It's the American way, naturally. Who would want to deny minority rights? And you've got to give them credit—they know exactly how to pull on our heartstrings and to capitalize on our better instincts. Who among us wants to be intolerant, or even *appear* to be?

Enter, then, the matter of *religious* tolerance. Should we not also be tolerant of all religious faiths? If the campus generation has been convinced that "political correctness" demands tolerance of such illegitimate interests as abortion, gay rights, and radical feminism, "political correctness" could, and should, demand religious tolerance.

But here it's important to remember what is meant by "tolerance" in a relativist society. It doesn't mean what it used to mean: permitting each person the right to believe (or disbelieve) according to his or her own conscience. That would be a respect for religious freedom far too noble for a secular society bent on the eradication of religious faith. In sharp contrast, today's "tolerance" means having to accept all values, truths, and beliefs (no matter how spiritually or morally bankrupt) as equally valid.

In such a "politically correct" climate, then, who would dare challenge religions which do not honor Jesus Christ? Or speak out against abortion and homosexuality? Or question whether someone's faith in Christ is complete without baptism? Or even mildly suggest that God may have called men and women to different role responsibilities in the church and in the home? These challenges are simply no longer acceptable. Besides being intolerant, they are anti-intellectual, unsophisticated, and altogether unAmerican!

And don't kid yourself into thinking that the day will never come when more than the *sensitivity* police will be enforcing such "political correctness." Liberal "tolerance" (like religious bigotry) has a nasty way of becoming enforced *intolerance* against all who disagree.

It's alarming enough to see "political correctness" being enforced among non-Christians. It's all the more chilling to witness it among ourselves. In a recent Bible lectureship, one of the more progressive-thinking speakers introduced a fairly novel idea for our fellowship, one which he knew was pretty radical for most in the audience. "Does this thought make you nervous?" he asked. *"Then get over it!"* he insisted. He might as well have said, "If you don't run along with the rest of us in the fast lane of progressive theology, you will henceforth be considered 'politically incorrect.'"

I only hope and pray that there is not an elite vanguard of influence brokers bent on imposing the latest "political correctness" in the church through "liberalism by fiat." The things that need changing in our fellowship deserve better than enforced conformity.

What all this portends for faith and doctrine should be amply clear. In the climate of "political correctness," even how we understand the Bible is under threat of being radically changed. Any hermeneutic which insists on the authoritativeness of Scripture is, by definition, politically incorrect. It's not sufficiently tolerant. It dares to set one standard above all others, or even to suggest that there are any standards whatever. When it comes to being politically correct, "command, example, and necessary inference" couldn't be more hopelessly outdated!

And, of course, such a hermeneutic is all the more politically incorrect when it leads us to doctrinal positions which themselves are out of step with what is "politically correct" according to the liberal agenda. For example, what could be more politically *incorrect* for the cultural church than maintaining the biblical pattern of male spiritual leadership? Surely, any hermeneutic that would lead us to such a "politically incorrect" doctrine *can't* be right. It is intolerant *per se.* And that forces some people to but one conclusion: Such a hermeneutic must be gotten rid of!

The call for a new hermeneutic does not arise in a vacuum. It is part of a larger, cultural ultimatum. Whether or not we are aware of it, political correctness is as much a part of the cultural church as it is the college campus. And heaven help us when what we have is the cultural church *on* a college campus! No prizes for guessing why the call for a new hermeneutic comes most aggressively from some of our own church-related universities, nor that it has its greatest appeal among those of the campus generation.

Toward a Utilitarian Hermeneutic

In vain, I keep looking for a definitive model or fully-articulated statement of what everyone seems to be calling the "new hermeneutic." My suspicion is that there is a move afoot either 1) simply to discard the "old hermeneutic" or 2) to address other significant issues only tenuously related to the hermeneutics question itself. Yet if there *were* a "new hermeneutic" floating around somewhere, I think I have an idea what it might look like.

From listening to my students, I am almost certain that there is a tie between the "new morality" and the call for a "new hermeneutic." That tie is what philosophers might call "utilitarian" morality. "Utilitarian morality" simply asks, "What works?" Nothing more, nothing less. For those who lack religious faith (and, sadly, for many who claim it), if abortion "works" for you, then it is "right." If homosexuality "works" for you, then it also is "right."

For society at large, what "works" is determined either by

majority rule or something very much akin to "might makes right." The political correctness movement demonstrates just how powerful special interest groups have become. If you have a sufficient power base, then "might makes right" even if you happen to be very much in the minority.

Just as the "new morality" is utilitarian, so, too, I suspect, is the call for a new hermeneutic. Undoubtedly, a utilitarian approach to faith and doctrine represents the thinking of many Christians in the cultural church. Where culture has turned from abstract right and wrong to a practical utilitarian ethic, you can bet that the cultural church is not far behind.

Two examples may help to illustrate what I mean by a "utilitarian hermeneutic." First, when I hear rumblings today about introducing instrumental music into our worship, the reason given for it has nothing to do with a re-examination of Scripture. Invariably, the reason is tied to declining attendance figures. "How are we going to keep the young people interested if we don't liven up our worship?" comes the plea. It's simply a matter of practicality; a matter of utility. Perhaps a matter of *effectiveness*, like song leaders, youth ministers, and even air-conditioning. We have a problem, and instrumental music just might be the solution. Discussion ended. Case closed.

A second example follows the same path. This time it relates to the controversy over an expanded role for women in the work and worship of the church. Once again, for some among us, it has less to do with any studied re-examination of Scripture on the issue than meeting a perceived need. What one hears over and over is the none-too-subtle justification: "If we don't allow women greater participation in the worship, we'll lose them—especially the younger ones— to other churches."

The problem which always plagues any utilitarian approach is the question of just how truly practical the idea happens to be. Instrumental music, for example, *might* attract young people to the worship; then again, it *might not*. Is it really *a cappella* music that's turning the young people off, or is it a church that no longer has any idea why it exists? Young people are rarely fooled by cosmetic changes. Besides, what you might gain among young people you might just as easily lose among the older folks who likely won't stand for trendy guitars and drums in the worship.

Likewise, gender equality in the church *might* prevent an exodus of the younger professional women; then again it *might not.* Is it really the principle of male spiritual leadership that's turning Christian women off, or is it the lack of spiritual leadership by any number of elders who have no clue what spiritual leadership is all about? And, of course, we're only kidding ourselves if we think that being socially conscious enough to "allow" women to pass communion trays or to read the scripture during the worship hour is going to satisfy their perceived need for greater inclusion. (I, too, would find that to be a demeaning compromise.) Besides, what you might gain among some women you might just as easily lose when others (both men and women) can no longer conscientiously join in the worship.

Practical solutions invariably tend to present their own practical problems. A utilitarian hermeneutic is not to be confused with a utopian hermeneutic. (What more proof do we need than the dwindling membership in churches which are leading the way in the women's movement?)

More important by far, of course, is the real reason why a utilitarian hermeneutic is misguided. It simply doesn't stop to ask what God thinks about whatever question is of concern. If there is anything of which we can be certain from a careful study of the Bible, it is that God does not operate on the basis of majority rule or power politics.

Nor is God pleased with an attitude which asks no further question beyond "What works?" Need we have a talk with Nadab and Abihu (who made an offering using unauthorized fire[2]), or perhaps Uzzah (who took God's law into his own hands when moving the ark of the Lord[3])? Even if these episodes have been overworked, their message still deserves our attention. What their fatal experiences with "practicality thinking" cost them might be well worth some serious reflection. They would have done far better to reject what in each instance amounted to "utilitarian hermeneutics."

If You Don't Like the Messenger...

A utilitarian view of the world—or, even more so, morality and doctrine—has devastating consequences. The ease with which some would cast aside the "old hermeneutic" is itself a demonstration of utilitarian thinking. If the "old hermeneutic" no longer "works" for us, then obviously it has to go!

But the real question is, Why does the "old hermeneutic" no longer "work" for us? Among those who have joined in the call for a new hermeneutic, the people whose judgment I value most are concerned about an overemphasis on church organization and function and a widespread neglect of teaching about sin and salvation and our spiritual relationship with God.

The greater concern at this point has to do with those in the cultural church who are demanding a new hermeneutic for all the wrong reasons—those whose interest in finding a new hermeneutic is more self-serving than theological. Call me suspicious, but I can't help but wonder at the *timing* of their interest in the hermeneutics question. Its current connection with one issue in particular is just too obvious for there to be mere coincidence. If you haven't already guessed from the many previous references, that issue is the so-called "women's issue."

Without the "women's issue," the question of a new hermeneutic would never have become so vital to some among us. At least not at this time. At least not in the *way* that it has. Undoubtedly, the spirit of the age eventually would have prompted a break between the cultural church and the authority of Scripture, and it is likely that more scholarly concerns about "the old hermeneutic" (which predate the "women's issue") eventually would have surfaced anyway. But it is the specific issue of the role of women that has provided the immediate catalyst and popularized the issue. Other issues, like the resurgent interest in instrumental music, are also part of the cultural church's hidden agenda, but none of them has the same capacity to be the driving engine behind the movement for radical change.

The "women's issue" is a perfect catalyst, because it combines utilitarian practicality, current notions of political correctness, and an obvious case for tolerance—all in one neat package. Madison Avenue could hardly wish for a more marketable product! And here is its connection with hermeneutics: Those who support a wider role for women have little choice but to get rid of the "old hermeneutic." Taking "command, example, and necessary inference" seriously would mean having to accept the well-documented biblical principle of male spiritual leadership at face value.

Hardly any biblical principle is more clearly established than the principle of male spiritual leadership. It begins at Creation, with Adam being created before Eve—a preview of the responsibility for leadership which would later be thrust upon all firstborn sons. As first *created*, Adam became the prototype husband, father, and family leader. Even in the consequences attendant upon their sin of disobedience, Eve is told: "Your desire will be for your husband, and he will rule over you."[4]

As we move to God's covenant with Abraham—a covenant to be shared by all his descendants, both male and female—we see God choosing as a symbol of the covenant the most exclusively male symbol possible: circumcision.[5] It was also God who instructed Moses regarding what was to be an all-male priesthood for the people of Israel.[6] Even when a woman, Deborah, led Israel as one of the judges, her message was one of rebuke, aimed at the men of Israel who had reneged on their leadership responsibility.[7]

Jesus, too, brought a message in his appointment of twelve men as apostles, despite the obvious availability of capable godly women. And the early church followed suit, appointing only men when certain special needs of the church arose.[8]

If there were ever any doubt, all doubt is removed, of course, by the specific teachings of the apostle Paul, who reminds us that "the head of the woman is man"[9]; that wives are to "submit to their husbands as to the Lord"[10]; and that women are not "to teach or to have authority over a man."[11]

The strength of the overwhelming documentation for the principle of male spiritual leadership is found in the massive effort which has been made to discount male headship teaching—especially the straightforward, clear-cut instructions delivered by the apostle Paul. Despite all the effort, dismissing Paul's teaching on the basis that it merely reflects archaic patriarchal notions and first century custom invariably fails, and fails miserably.

Paul makes it clear that male spiritual leadership is neither cultural nor merely patriarchal, but is God-ordained "because of the angels"[12] (whatever that might mean), because "it was the woman who was deceived"[13] (whatever that means), and because "Adam was formed first"[14] (however we might understand that). If there are explanations that challenge our best thinking, nevertheless the basic message is clear: Male spiritual leadership is God's idea—not man's.

When the attempt to discredit Paul's prohibitive instructions proves futile, the alternative tactic is to make Paul out to be a schizophrenic good guy/bad guy. Galatians 3:28 is paraded out in a desperate last-ditch effort to find role equality from Paul's statement that, in Christ, we are "neither male nor female."[15] It hardly seems to matter that the proper context is totally obliterated by many of the same people who are most vocal in their insistence that the "old hermeneutic" wrests individual scriptures out of context in a mad dash to reach desired doctrinal results!

The Sophistication of Cultural Arguments

By contrast with the transparent abuse of Galatians 3:28, a far more subtle argument is being made. Superficially, it has the look of a biblically-based perspective, but it is cultural to the core. As articulated by a leader in one of the more progressive congregations:

> Paul regulated (but did not explicitly abolish) slavery and male domination in his own time, and for the very same reason in each instance: so as not to hinder the gospel's spread by an abrupt break with culture. However, the apostle decisively sowed the seeds which eventually would grow into the abolition of both institutions. It would seem that faithfulness to Paul's missionary *principles* now call for a reversal of his actual *applications*, since moral sensitivities of the larger culture today

are offended by both slavery and by the subjugation of women and an insistence on either
would tend to hinder the gospel's credibility and
spread.

This sophisticated statement—subtly mixing together
both first century culture and today's culture in one lethal
cocktail—is an excellent illustration of the cultural influence
that has swayed so many among our number today. But a
closer look reveals gaping holes in its logic.

First and foremost, it fails to recognize that slavery as an
institution was never commanded, whereas male spiritual
leadership is expressly taught and commanded throughout
the whole of Scripture. Moreover, the supposed parallel
between slavery and gender role distinctions breaks down
immediately, considering that regulation of *children* accompanied the regulations for both women and slaves.[16] If
women and slaves were meant to be in the same category of
liberation, are we to take it that, in a culture which increasingly honors "juvenile rights," children are no longer obli-
gated to obey their parents?

The argument also ignores Paul's *specifically-stated reasons* for his teachings on gender distinctions, which have
much to do with "Adam being formed first," and "because of
the angels," but not even a hint of any so-called "missionary
principle."

Of course, there is also the assumption—made through
the eyes of radical feminism—that gender role distinctions
are a form of "subjugation" (and tantamount to slavery?). If
the biblical concept of "submission" bears this connotation,
then we must all ignore Paul's direction that we "submit to
one another out of reverence to Christ."[17] Use of the word
"subjugation" in the place of "submission" demonstrates how
even terms are re-defined through the lexicon of culture.

This highly inventive explanation also overlooks other
"abrupt breaks with culture" which were never watered down
for the sake of missionary success. Consider, for example,
the abrupt break with Jewish circumcision and the equally
abrupt break with such Gentile practices as the eating of
blood, or of food sacrificed to idols. Each of these abrupt
breaks with culture could have hindered (indeed, in some

cases, *did* hinder) the spread of the gospel.

Finally, such a culturally-correct perspective puts the gospel and evangelism at the mercy of "cultural sensitivity." What does that sensitivity suggest for evangelism within a culture which would be offended by any doctrine which might be considered homophobic? If the spread of the gospel is hindered by condemning homosexuality, should we simply abandon the scriptural teaching against it in favor of some greater "missionary principle?"

The cultural argument relative to both the first century and today can look very appealing. But somehow, some way, we must break through the superficial sophistication of the cultural argument and see it for what it really is: an accommodation to culture first; a faithful response to scriptural teaching only a distant second.

The Impact on Hermeneutics

The plain truth is that a careful understanding of Scripture simply will not support gender-role sameness. Virtually from cover to cover, the Bible announces, stresses, demonstrates, and repeats all over again that God has created man and woman equally in his own image—equal in worth, equal in value, equal in service—but with unique role responsibilities in which man is appointed to spiritual leadership. It's almost impossible to miss it!

But, for the moment, it is more important that we understand just how fundamentally the "women's issue" has challenged our way of understanding the Bible. When we consider the principle of male spiritual leadership, we find it taught in the form of "commands" ("I do not permit a woman to teach..."); "examples" (male priesthood, male apostles, even a male Messiah); and "inferences" (such as elders being male, as suggested by the directive that they be "husbands of but one wife"[18]).

Given the clear weight of evidence against gender-role sameness when the Bible is objectively read through the eyes of "command, example, and necessary inference," the cultural church finds itself in a quandary: The message itself is clear and unequivocal; but the message is not one we want to hear. So what are we to do? Given our cultural commitment to tolerance, utility, and political correctness, we have no other choice. In order to avoid hearing the message, we're going to have to shoot the messenger! And the messenger in this case is the "old hermeneutic."

"Give us another messenger," cries the cultural church. Give us a new hermeneutic that will permit us more freedom. Give us a new hermeneutic that doesn't bind us to legalistic doctrine, inductive reasoning, scientific method, simplistic blueprints, sterile constitutions, or common sense understanding of God's Word. Give us *anything* that will affirm our commitment to cultural thinking and justify the conclusions we have already reached.

If possible, of course, make it *sound* spiritual—perhaps a "hermeneutic of the cross." Dress it up in culturally-acceptable terms like *justice* and *equality*, and be sure to throw in a generous helping of biblical *love*. Make it look sufficiently respectable, and maybe no one will notice that what we've really done is to abandon scriptural authority.

So the messenger was killed and the cultural church roared its approval: "The 'old hermeneutic' is dead! Long live the 'new hermeneutic!'"

Worse Than Simply Weighing Anchor

Among the many criticisms of the "old hermeneutic" is that it tends to have a "leveling effect" on the whole of Scripture. That is, it tends to overlook any distinction between the *core message* of the gospel (Christ's death, burial, and resurrection) and everything else which is *secondary* (like church organization and function). To the extent that we have "majored in minors," the criticism is valid. But there is every potential for a far more dangerous "leveling effect" when we play fast and loose with hermeneutics.

Missing, avoiding, or blatantly rejecting the principle of male spiritual leadership may well lead to ruinous consequences far beyond more immediate questions of *Who* can do *What* in the assembly of the church. But even those ruinous consequences are penny-ante compared with the disaster which lurks in the wake of any radical change in the way we understand the Bible.

When you undermine the authority of Scripture in order to resolve any one particular doctrinal issue, you undermine it on every front, whether it be "secondary" matters like the work and worship of the church, or even the "core message" of the gospel. Credibility has its own "domino effect." Push the first one over, and they all fall down—primary and secondary, "essential" and "non-essential" alike. If we can't trust Paul on the role of men and women in the church, how can we trust him on baptism and the Lord's supper?

What's happening in the call for a new hermeneutic is nothing short of what's happening in the "new morality." It is not simply "doctrinal decline" on a given church issue that we are experiencing. Today we are facing the very real prospect of abandoning altogether our commitment to biblical authority. That is the reason the hermeneutics question is so vital to our fellowship. It threatens to divide us, not merely on the role of women or whatever else might be of current controversy, but over our most basic assumptions.

And divide us it will. All you have to do is to look at the Disciples of Christ, for example, to see that the single issue of instrumental music was not the sole, or even the key factor in our parting of the ways. Today, the Disciples of Christ are as different from us in their view of scriptural authority as any other mainstream denomination which never shared our restorationist roots.

What happened back then is happening again now. It's a battle over how we are to understand Scripture. It's a test of our respect for biblical authority. Future generations will look back to the cultural church at the end of the twentieth century and know which direction we took at the fork in the road.

It's dangerous enough to weigh anchor on an issue here or an issue there. Drifting doctrinally always begs disaster. But, if we do no more than inadvertently drift away from our moorings, by the grace of God we can always come to our senses and lower the anchor once again.

It's another thing altogether to *leave our anchor behind!* And that is essentially what we are risking in the call for a new hermeneutic. Is that what we really want? Have we become so comfortable *drifting* on one matter of doctrine after another that we have decided to jettison our anchor altogether, like so much excess baggage?

I wish you could sit in on one of my Law and Morality classes. The frantic struggle of some of today's brightest minds to parrot the politically correct party line and yet avoid the obvious moral absurdities when that line is pushed to its logical extreme is not a pretty picture. You just know that on their way home from class they are asking themselves, "Did I *really* say that?"

As victims of the "new morality" (which is no morality at all), they face a directionless future, set adrift in a sea of moral uncertainty. They have nothing to which they can confidently anchor their beliefs. Yet what their "new morality" is doing for them is not so different from what the cultural church's new hermeneutic will do for us if we're not extremely careful. It promises greater freedom in Christ and an enhanced sense of spirituality, but guarantees only aimless self-determination in a sea of spiritual uncertainty.

SEVEN

Rationalizing The Irrational

If you believe in the Gospel what you like, and reject what you don't like, it is not the Gospel you believe, but yourself.
—St. Augustine of Hippo

Spurred by the interest of an out-of-town visitor, I found myself browsing skeptically at the whimsical contemporary paintings and sculptures displayed in the 20th Century room of the Norton Simon Museum of Art in Pasadena. "Whimsical" is my word for: "Are you kidding? You're seriously telling me this stuff is really *art*?" Thankfully, my time spent in trying to figure out the deep meanings of totally bizarre attempts at artistic expression did not go unrewarded. On the wall near the entrance to the room, I discovered an explanation of surrealist art that was worth the price of admission.

If you are not familiar with the term *surrealist art*, it's what many people might speak of as *modern* art or *pop* art (though not precisely correct). It tends to be art which borders on the bizarre, the fanciful, even the outrageous. Not quite sure myself as to what all it encompassed, I was intrigued by the explanation on the gallery wall. Under the wary eye of a suspicious museum guard, I hastily scrawled the following words:

> As a rule, a surrealistic composition combines elements from realities that are obvious and elements that contradict ordinary visible reality. This may be no more complex than the combination of two different realities, such as a

photo from two negatives, or a tea cup covered with fur. The artist thus creates an image which is designed to disorient ordinary assumption patterns. *The purpose is to propel the viewer out of the realm of logical mind into the realm of intuitive mind.* The resulting composition can be described as an "*impossible reality.*"

You're probably asking yourself, What in the world does "a tea cup covered with fur" have to do with how we should understand Scripture! Yet, incredibly enough, I suspect that this unlikely definition aptly explains much of the current demand for a new hermeneutic. Far from being a matter of abstract theology, the hermeneutic question reflects a more wide-spread major shift in the way that we think.

How we think today is as dramatically different as the 20th Century room was from the Renaissance and European rooms just down the hall. More than time had passed between the old masters and today's pop artists. It was not just a matter of centuries. With the passing of time has come a whole new way of looking at our universe. With the 20th century has come not only the various revolutions—from scientific to political to art—but a revolution in basic life assumptions, truths, and values. Our shared perception of God, religion, authority—even the idea of truth itself—has changed. How else could our minds accommodate a phrase like "impossible reality?" It, too, is surreal—*un*real!

Into the New Age Mind

I first encountered "impossibility reality" as a philosophical point-of-view when I began my investigation into the New Age movement. Much of New Age belief is about paranormal experiences—as in *not* normal or *beyond* the norm. Specifically, as in "astral projections" (claimed out-of-body experiences), "channeling" (where psychics supposedly go into a trance and turn into a kind of "human telephone" so that you can talk to disembodied spirits "out there" somewhere), and extraterrestrials (something like the film-goers' lovable E.T., but *for real*!).

It sounded crazy to me, and I assumed it sounded crazy to everyone else, except perhaps to a few left-over acid-brained hippies from the sixties. To my surprise, I discovered that all this sounded entirely plausible to a large number of doctors, lawyers, and other mainstream professionals on whose sound judgment we normally would rely for the most important of our affairs.

Of course, these same people can stand on the beach at the edge of the Pacific—unable to stop the oncoming rush of the tide or to keep the sun from setting at the end of the day—yet confidently shout out to the heavens: "I am God! I am God! I am God!" Talk about "impossible reality" in the realm of religious faith!

Should it be surprising, then, that one of the central beliefs of New Age teaching is that rational thought is hopelessly outdated, one-dimensional, and therefore limiting? Surely, you've heard all the right-brain/left-brain psychobabble. The left side of the brain supposedly thinks rationally; the right side, intuitively. (Did the left side rationally *decide* that distinction, or did the right side *intuit* it?) Of course, the call of the New Age is to abandon the left side's "masculine rationality" in favor of the right side's "feminine intuition," which is more creative, sensitive, emotional, harmonious, and insightful.

The tie between rationality and masculinity ought to be as offensive to women as to men (irrationality a *feminine* trait?), but it is women who most often press the distinction. In that regard, it should not be surprising that 1) now is the time when a wider role for women in the church is being urged, and 2) much of the justification for that shift is found in bitter rejection of patriarchal (masculine) and "legalistic" (rational, left-brain) thinking.

Would that these were the only implications for the church, but the bad news gets worse. We once thought that faith in the unseen was based rationally upon evidence of that which is seen. Today's message is that faith need not be rational in any sense, at any point. We can believe whatever feels good. Extraterrestrial visitors in spaceships? If it feels good to you, believe it! Past lives as the king of France, or as an elephant or a tree? Why not! A philosophically inconsistent belief in both Hinduism and Christianity? Go for it!

Nothing we believe anymore need have any rational content, and logical fallacies are of no consequence.

Is it any wonder that a belief system allowing for totally illogical faith should aggressively encourage its followers to abandon rationality in favor of intuition? Or any wonder that the purpose of 20th century surrealist art is to "propel the viewer out of the realm of *logical* mind into the realm of *intuitive* mind"? Or that the cultural church is urging us to abandon the objectivity of "command, example, and necessary inference" in favor of a more subjective/intuitive "love story between us and God"?

I'm not suggesting that anyone is consciously urging that we actually abandon all reason. There's too much reasoned argument being marshalled in favor of a hermeneutical change. However, I see more and more evidence that suggests rational minds are being put to work in an effort to avoid the impact of certain scriptures which are considered to be culturally or theologically offensive. In the struggle over the "role of women," for example, many today effectively are elevating the intuitive mind over the rational mind.

For many, it's kind of a love/hate syndrome: We love rationalism when it matches our own conception of God's truth, but hate rationalism if it tells us that what we want to do is wrong. The difficulty in recognizing the "hate" part is that invariably it appears incognito, looking for all the world like "love." "What would *Jesus* do today?" we are asked, for example, regarding the role of women—as if we could somehow intuitively come up with a "loving" answer that would be different from a rational understanding of Scripture which tells us what Jesus, in fact, *did* do (as in appointing only men to be his apostles).

On the surface, asking what Jesus would do certainly *sounds* right. However, it can become a subtle way of replacing the rational, objective pursuit of what he did do, and can prevent our asking *why* he did it, and what implications that might have for us today. I find it interesting that, regarding this issue in particular, these questions are not being asked by those who would urge a more Christ-centered hermeneutic. Is our asking what sounds like the right question merely providing an opportunity for covering over our preferences with a thin veneer of religious authority?

Where the New Age movement leans toward the intuitive in order to rationalize the irrational, are we also wanting to abandon a logical hermeneutic in order to rationalize doing what we intuitively feel is right for the church, even though rationally understood Scripture would lead us in a different direction? If so, we may find ourselves replacing the logic of revealed Scripture with the illogic of either the *psycho*-logical (subjectivism) or the *socio*-logical (culturalism). When push comes to shove, everyone follows a certain logic—be it one kind or another. The only question is whether we are following God's logic or our own. Are we reading Scripture with a consistent, coherent approach, or with a selective, subjective approach?

A Rationality That May Make No Sense

Of course, the "logic of Scripture" is not to be equated with human logic. Spiritual thinking is seldom consistent with our natural way of thinking. When it comes to knowing the mind of God, that which is truly spiritual makes no earthly sense. For, as Jeremiah reminds us, "it is not for man to direct his steps."[1] Or as Solomon puts it, "There is a way that seems right to a man, but in the end it leads to death."[2] Little wonder, then, that Solomon leaves us with this admonition: "Trust in the Lord with all your heart and lean not on your own understanding; in all your ways acknowledge him, and he will make your paths straight."[3]

Is Solomon telling us to park our logic and intuitively feel our way to God? Hardly! We're not to lean on our own understanding, whether rational *or* intuitive! Jesus put it into perspective: "Love the Lord your God with all your heart and with all your soul and with all your mind."[4] If the heart is intuitive, the mind is meant to be rational. The beauty of Creation is that God gave us both heart *and* mind with which to embrace him.

The point is that godly faith can be found by a person with an open heart through a rational process of seeking to understand divine revelation; but that our rational pursuit of truth may lead us to what human rationality, if taken alone, would often consider to be illogical. What better example than Jesus' own post-resurrection appearance to the eleven?

After defying human logic by appearing miraculously in their midst, Jesus "opened their *minds* so they could *understand* the Scriptures."[5] If we have minds open to truth, then our minds, like theirs, are capable of rationally understanding the message of God's revelation.

At its outer limits, of course, human rationality can but scratch the surface of God's mind. "Oh, the depth of the riches of the wisdom and knowledge of God! How unsearchable his judgments, and his paths beyond tracing out!"[6] But to give up on the rational, logical pursuit of truth is to nullify the mystery "now revealed and made known through the prophetic writings by the command of the eternal God, so that all nations might believe and obey him."[7]

God's logic and man's logic are not at all on the same plane. But make no mistake. To know the mind of God is to be rational, for God's laws are both full of reason and accessible to reason.

Postmodern Relativism

The New Age thinking of our generation is really nothing more than unabashed relativism, only packaged more slickly than ever before. The wrapping on today's package is called *postmodernism,* a rather daunting word almost defying definition. Loosely speaking, it refers to the end of the "modern" period begun by the Enlightenment rationalists—generally regarded as a scientific, mind-oriented world view—and its replacement by a less scientific, more heart-oriented world view. Where "modernism" appealed to logic, postmodernism appeals to more sensory, experience-related perceptions.

If I were to give a totally biased definition of postmodernism, it would be that we've simply grown out of one kind of pride (human rationalism) into another kind of pride (human intuition). As we will see in Chapter 9, there was never really much difference in the first place. It's just that now our culture is more up front about it. We're no longer ashamed to admit what we're up to.

Postmodernism really means that we are now too sophisticated to believe in any objective, knowable, universal, absolute, capital-"T" truth out there. The only truth we acknowledge is the fact that we *can't* know truth—at least not for sure, at least not for everyone, at least not for all time. And we can't really even know this for a *fact*, because there are no "facts." "Facts" are based upon objective reality known by scientific method—an anathema in religious matters, so we are told, to be avoided at all cost.

In what has to be one of the greatest perversions of all time, more than one writer among us has condemned as *idolatrous* anyone today who determinedly sets out to marshall "facts" (Scripture) toward the goal of grasping a fundamentally mysterious reality (the mind of God). "How dare a person be so vain as to think that he can rationally discover that which is truly spiritual!"

The bizarre finger-pointing going on here boggles the mind! It would be one thing to be reminded of Jesus' rebuke to those who would "diligently study the Scriptures because you think that by them you possess eternal life."[8] Neither Scripture *as Scripture*, nor any hermeneutic, is the ultimate source of our life with God. It is Christ himself. But it is altogether outrageous to suggest that one who prayerfully and systematically searches the sacred Scriptures is trying to save himself by his own ingenuity!

If it is Self and Self's reason that are the claimed objects of this disguised idolatry, why would such a self-directed person even bother to join with the Bereans in their noble search of the Scriptures? And why seek for truth, if one already knows the truth?

The cultural church's plea for a new hermeneutic that acknowledges the limits of human reason is wrapped in bundles of false humility. It confesses the obvious—that we can never, by any method or formula, fully grasp the revealed text—and then blithely excludes any biblical passage which doesn't seem to stand well at the foot of the cross. Where better to mask our pride, of course, than at the foot of the cross!

But we must not forget that when we claim to stand at the foot of the cross we are under the watchful gaze of the Man of Judgment who will not be fooled in the least if our presence at his feet is merely a photo opportunity. Who but Christ himself can ever know, but I get the distinct feeling that, for many, the quest for a new hermeneutic is less associated with the humility of the cross ("*Thy* will be done") and more closely linked with a prideful "*My* will be done."

That is what the postmodern mind is all about: *my* perception; *my* understanding; *my* reality. "Reality" in postmodernism—just as "reality" in the New Age movement—is whatever you perceive it to be, looking from your own unique perspective.

When Einstein discovered relativity physics (which is scientifically valid), he unwittingly ushered in an era of relativity hermeneutics (which is neither scientific nor valid). It's one thing to say that where you happen to stand as an observer changes how you perceive a given distant object (relativity physics); it is another thing altogether to say that there is therefore no absolute truth in Scripture—that it's all in the eye of the beholder (relativity hermeneutics). Little wonder that our interpretation of the Bible is up for grabs—everybody to his or her own liking, however we happen to see it, no one way being any better than any other way.

And the discovery of quantum mechanics in the field of physics was not just about chaos in subatomic particles (interestingly known as "the *uncertainty* principle"), but has been transformed into uncertainty in morals, doctrine, and faith.

What a wild ride we have taken from the days when order in the universe was routinely offered as proof of God's creative genius and power; to the discovery that at the minutest levels of the universe there is apparent disorder; to the incredible conclusion that, therefore, our universe is not as orderly as we once thought and that, therefore (gasp!), there may not really be a God out there after all, much less morality or true biblical doctrine! Should we be surprised that "scriptural authority" no longer has the same tinge of urgency it once had? If God himself is in doubt, what chance does his revelation have, much less its authority over us?

Given all of this, it's hardly surprising that postmodernism presents us with a strange blending of the scientific with the mystical, the intellectual with an almost evangelistic anti-intellectualism.

Of course, all the postmodern talk about relativity physics and quantum mechanics presents us with yet more irony. Science itself is being used to justify the very kind of non-scientific, postmodern values which have validated the cultural church's call for a "new hermeneutic."

Naturally, in an age when there is no longer any such thing as "contradiction," hardly anyone takes notice of the ironies. A scientific method which allows everyone to choose his or her own reality (shorthand for doctrine and morals) is truly heaven-sent and not to be questioned!

In this regard, of course, not even the cross, as some have suggested, can be a fail-safe hermeneutic. For, in the spirit of postmodernism, the cross means all things to all people. Some folks outside our fellowship see nothing but *love* looking down from the cross, and are therefore convinced that Jesus would never be so unloving as to exclude practicing homosexuals from the pulpit. What others see in Christ's sacrifice on the cross is a call for divine *justice*, and are therefore sure that no one is really going to hell (the belief in universalism). Sadly, when you hear the phrase "justice-love" being referred to today, you can almost bet that something unbiblical is being promoted.

How is it possible that the bad guys can always hijack good terminology and turn it into something unworthy? *Gay* was a perfectly good word before homosexual activists appropriated it for themselves. And so was (and still is) the *atonement* of Christ's blood on the cross before New Agers hyphenated it to death in blasphemously proclaiming their "at-one-ment" with God. Now we have to concern ourselves with a whole new gloss which some are giving to a *hermeneutic of the cross*.

In 1 Corinthians 11, Paul offers the cross to explain the significance of the Lord's supper, and in Romans 6 he returns to the cross for a picture of what baptism is all about. That is what a "hermeneutic of the cross" ought to be about. But at the hands of more and more among us today, the meaning of such a hermeneutic has been hijacked and misappropriated.

A more manipulable "hermeneutic of the cross" is beginning to cast its highly subjective shadow beyond Calvary, putting even such subjects as baptism and the Lord's supper in jeopardy. We're already hearing the early rumblings, and who knows when the floodgate will be unleashed: "Would the Christ of the cross really make a fuss about regular observance of the Lord's supper?" And, "What would the Christ of the cross say about those who believe in him but fail to grasp the significance of being baptized?"

Yet perhaps it is the very idea of *truth itself* that has become our problem in this postmodern era. Has truth simply succumbed to culture? Would the Spirit of *truth*[9] be welcomed into our worship assemblies today, or is it only the "spirit of the times" to whom we eagerly extend the hand of fellowship?

Under a hermeneutic that is more culturally sensitive than biblically sensitive, meaning and understanding of Scripture can be no more than an illusive mirage, incapable of being grasped. For with each change in culture comes a new context, and with each change in context comes a new truth. In the ever-changing truths of postmodern thought, there is simply no room for Him who once hung on the cross, Jesus Christ—"the same yesterday and today and forever."[10]

The Popular Art of Spontaneous Unreasoning

When I think back on my visit to the Norton Simon Museum, it strikes me that the art of the old masters was a study in realism, focusing (not at all coincidentally) upon one biblical scene after another. And, although each painting expressed the artist's own intuitive feeling of the scene being depicted, the invariable result was a recognizable representation of the essential truth of that which was being portrayed. Renaissance art was itself a commonly pursued hermeneutic which realistically interpreted the biblical story.

The fact that contemporary art rarely, if ever, even attempts to depict the biblical story is its own telling commentary on the "spirit of our times." But suppose contemporary art were asked to attempt an interpretation of the cross, or perhaps the open tomb. What image might result? Left to a "surrealist hermeneutic," you can bet that logic would be distorted by an appeal to the intuitive, and the odds are that the resulting picture would be nothing like the true biblical story. In fact, the more outrageous and shocking the better! (Consider, for example, the recent controversy over Andres Serrano's taxpayer-supported photograph of a crucifix immersed in the artist's urine.)

For those who sincerely search for a hermeneutic that will give us a truer picture of the biblical story, I pass along one final caution. As I was leaving the exhibit of contemporary art, two words caught my attention. They were the words of S. W. Hayter (1901-1988) giving his classic definition of the surrealist technique of automism. The words? "Spontaneous unreasoning!"

I'll be among the first to concede that our often distorted use of "the old hermeneutic" has not always given us the truest possible picture of the biblical story, if for no other reason than that we have tended to concern ourselves more with head coverings, *a cappella* voices, and qualified elders than with the cross of Christ and his open tomb. But giving up a rational (realist) hermeneutic in favor of some yet-to-be-defined postmodern interpretation runs every risk of falling prey to the irrational (surrealist) hermeneutic of our age, so succinctly and chillingly defined as "spontaneous unreasoning."

It's a time for honest reflection. In the call for a new hermeneutic, are we sincerely seeking a better way to understand the unfathomable mystery of our salvation, or are we simply being caught up in a postmodern generation that is intentionally and unashamedly losing its mind?

EIGHT

Looking At Others To See Ourselves

Every church is orthodox to itself; to others, erroneous, or heretical.

—John Locke

News Item: "Evangelical Christians," says Church of England's Archbishop George Carey, "have been guilty of treating the Bible in simplistic fashion, ignoring the historical, literary and cultural dimensions of this greatest of all books." Also today, Archbishop Carey joined forces with many of England's bishops in calling for the ordination of women.[1]

News Item: Director Roland Joffe, of *The Killing Fields* and *The Mission*, has just finished shooting *The City of Joy*, a film based on the life of a Calcutta rickshaw-puller, and in the process has raised a greater storm than even this city has seen.

Joffe tried to pre-empt "anti-racists" protests by meticulous research about Calcutta's slum life. Joffe realized early on that one of his problems in Calcutta was the very different perceptions.

"In the West we tend to be Cartesian, mechanical, legalistic. We believe there is a truth which stands whole and untarnished and we can build our conceptions on that. In Asia people are more interested in perceptions; that to them is the greater truth. The problem is that when I have tried to reach out to those who are criticizing my film we have constantly been tripping over our own cultures."[2]

News item: Some Protestant churches in Southern California are learning what Catholic parishes have known for two decades—that Saturday evening is a convenient option to Sunday morning services. The trend toward adding Saturday services "is a mounting wave, especially for growth-minded churches running out of seating and parking on Sunday morning," said the Rev. Scott Bauer, executive pastor for ministry at Church on the Way.

Starting the Sunday worship cycle on Saturday evening has been compared by clergy to Jewish holy day services held on the evening before and the morning after. "But the real reasons for the innovation are practical and social," Bauer said. "A straw poll told us that 10% to 12% of our congregation were unable to attend our Sunday morning services because of their work schedules."[3]

News item: Our [*Christianity Today* magazine] chart lumped Mormons and Jehovah's Witnesses with Southern Baptists for sociological, not theological reasons. Students of church growth recognize that these groups share a pattern of resisting cultural change (the breakdown of the two-parent family, for example) and of adhering to an authority of "supernatural" origin. The declining denominations, which we labeled "Liberal," adapt more quickly to social change, and (sadly) frequently fail to measure social forces against a transcendent authority.—Eds.[4]

News item: Next month, the General Assembly of the Presbyterian Church (USA) will be asked to adopt the report of the General Assembly Special Committee on Human Sexuality. Here is a sample of the report's pronouncements and recommendations:

*That "all persons, whether heterosexual or homosexual, whether single or partnered, have a moral right to experience justice-love in their lives and to be sexual persons."

*That gays and lesbians be received as full participant members, and for ordination, "regardless of their sexual orientation."

*That worship resources be designed to celebrate same-sex relationships.

*That the problem before the church is not sexual sin but the "prevailing social, cultural, and ecclesial arrangements...[and] conformity to the unjust norm of compulsory heterosexuality."[5]

Culturalism is a Universal Threat

From the above news items, three important points emerge to illuminate our discussion of hermeneutics in the churches of Christ. The first is that we are not alone in our struggle over how to understand the Bible. Other churches in the wider Christian community are equally perplexed, equally divided, and equally challenged. Sometimes the controversy emerges under headlines like "Southern Baptists Split Over Biblical Inerrancy" or "Church Storm Brewing Over Gender-Inclusive Lectionary." But whatever the particular issue, current shifts in doctrinal thinking are hardly limited to our fellowship.

That observation leads to the second point: that the so-called "hermeneutics issue" is principally one of culture, not abstract theology. As director Joffe vividly reminds us, it can be a cultural problem pure and simple, with no theology involved at any point. The more our New Age culture starts thinking like the mystical religions of Calcutta, the more difficulty we are going to have thinking rationally in any context. The problem is that culture stains everything that it touches—including matters as seemingly remote and untouchable as how we interpret the Bible.

Whereas restorationist roots are the target of growing criticism among our own fellowship, the truth is that other churches not sharing our restorationist roots are also facing either similar calls for a new hermeneutic or some other challenge to basic biblical authority. Churches having never heard of "command, example, and necessary inference" are asking many of the same questions we are now being asked.

The third point is raised by the recognition that this observation can cut two ways: 1)Either that our hermeneutic—like the hermeneutics of other churches—has become an unjust victim of a secularist culture, and is therefore not deserving of the current criticism being leveled against it; or 2) that, as people caught up in a materialistic, scientific, and rationalistic society, we have all come to our senses and are all recognizing the need to get back to an openness to transcendence and a more confessional faith.

Would that the latter were true, but, as the news items above graphically illustrate, the widespread call for a new hermeneutic is almost invariably accompanied, not by growth in spiritual transcendence, but by moral slippage. Following a now-familiar story line of liberty becoming license, it starts out innocently enough with such concerns as a wider role for women, but quickly degenerates into the legitimizing of such immoral activities as homosexuality. The anchor for church doctrine is the same as for personal morality. Leave Scripture behind in one area and you've left it behind in all areas.

The problem with a culturally-defined hermeneutic is that it cannot help but reflect the standards of culture. In terms of morals, much less doctrine, ours is no longer a culture to be trusted. Considering what is happening in churches around us when they abandon the authority of Scripture and soon find themselves at the bottom of a moral trash heap, the Hebrew writer's words take on added, if slightly different, significance: "Therefore, since we are surrounded by such a great cloud of witnesses, let us throw off everything that hinders and the sin that so easily entangles...."[6]

Broader Perspective, Or Shrunken Scripture?

To emphasize the wider impact of hermeneutical struggle throughout the entire Christian community, let me share with you the response of James R. Edwards, professor of religion at Jamestown College, to the Presbyterian church's controversy over its Human Sexuality committee report. It speaks equally well to our own fellowship:

> First, the report is an example of what happens when pluralism, rather than Scripture, is made the final arbiter of faith and morality. The report may claim a place of honor for Scripture, but, like the honor of the queen of England, it is largely a formality. Citing a shift away from "explicit appeals to scriptural authority" to "the broad message of

Scripture," the report reveals a reductionist view of Scripture. By "broad message," the committee means "inclusive wholeness" and all Scripture that challenges that canon is summarily omitted.

In the minds of the committee, the "historical distance between twentieth-century Christians and first-century Christians" is too great for us "to borrow...their conclusions about human sexuality."[7]

Does it take someone from outside our own back-to-the-Bible fellowship to remind us of the subtle sleight-of-hand that is going on when we are asked to get away from "neat lists of doctrine" and see "the broader picture"? Far from getting a "broader picture," what happens all too often is that any passage which proves to be an embarrassment is simply ignored. The result is that the impact of Scripture is not broadened at all, but rather is shrunk to just the right size to fit whatever hidden agenda we might wish to maintain. You aim to hit the "Enlarge" button, but end up pushing the "Reduce" button instead.

Pitfalls of a Pluralistic Hermeneutic

Another of Edwards' observations points up a major concern facing the cultural church. "The report," says Edwards, "is an example of what happens when pluralism, rather than Scripture, is made the final arbiter of faith and morality." It's the word *pluralism* that's important.

Pluralism, much like tolerance, is the belief that there should be universal acceptance of all thoughts, beliefs, and actions. But even beyond the more passive idea of tolerance, pluralism insists that there be an *active* inclusion of the entire community, no matter how morally decadent or doctrinally skewed any given part of it may be. Pluralism not only demands that we be gender-blind and color-blind, but also morally blind.

Pluralism has its own spirit—the spirit of *gratuitous accommodation*. That means going out of our way to please people simply for the sake of pleasing them—regardless of any moral or doctrinal implications. Pluralism is all about diversity (we must have it for its own sake). And pluralism is all about sensitivity. No prizes, of course, for guessing which culture has become the most sensitive lately.

Once pluralism becomes part of the cultural church, decisions must of necessity be made on a different basis than previously. The spirit of gratuitous accommodation asks not, "What is God telling us through his Word?" but rather, "How can we please most of the people most of the time?" The more diverse the make-up of the congregation, the more important pluralism becomes. And because we are a church wedded to culture, in the years to come we are likely to have greater and greater diversity, leading to more and more gratuitous accommodation.

There is a sense in which we can already observe pluralism in process, and even how it leads to the shrinking of Scripture. Take the matter of divorce, for example. The more members of a congregation who have been divorced (whether for "scriptural cause" or not), the less likely we are to hear sermons condemning unscriptural divorce.

To the contrary, typically, we will start hearing more sermons on "Growing Through Divorce," or "Healing the Hurt." Jesus' hard teaching about divorce[8] will be conveniently sidestepped as too offensive, at worst, and too sensitive, at the least. With that simple act of gratuitous accommodation in the pursuit of well-meaning pluralism, the Bible will have been curtly reduced by one third of a chapter. And so on it shrinks—chapter by chapter, sin by culturally-accepted sin, until none of us has to squirm anymore.

Those who are calling for a new hermeneutic must ask themselves some tough questions: Is it legalism that we're concerned about, or have we become converts to pluralism and its goal of accommodating whatever might be on culture's latest agenda? To what extent is the call for a new hermeneutic an expression of willingness to reduce Scripture, if necessary, in aid of a worthy cause?

The Siren Call of Cultural Conformity

When it comes to understanding ourselves by looking at others, there are wonderful lessons to be learned even from beyond the broader "Christian community." In his book, *Reform Judaism: A Historical Perspective,*[9] William G. Braude discusses early Jewish reformers in Germany. What he observes about them raises one of the most serious questions possible about the call for hermeneutical reform in today's cultural church. "Their reforms," says Braude, "were facilitated by the social, political, and intellectual climate of the times. The Jew had begun to move fearlessly among his gentile neighbors and, [emphasis mine] *to avoid conspicuousness, he clipped his beard....*"

Wow! What a statement! What a commentary on the pressures of cultural conformity. "*To avoid conspicuousness, he clipped his beard!*"

Ironically, the greater the call for pluralism (accommodating diversity), the more we are urged to conform. The greater the call for pluralism, the more we *want* to conform! It reminds me of the way young people usually dress. They are so desperate to be nonconformists that they all end up wearing the same things!

Nobody really wants to be different. At least nobody wants to be on the wrong side of the tracks. Certainly no one who *already is* on the wrong side wants to stay there if he can help it. Why, then, should we be surprised that we too want to "clip our beards" in order to be less conspicuous either in the world at large or among the wider "Christian community"?

Just think about it. In what ways are the churches of Christ different from the rest of the "Christian community"? (Unfortunately, we tend to concentrate negatively on how embarrassingly *different* we are rather than on how commendably *distinctive* we are.) Even before you get to a more substantive doctrine like adult believer baptism, the first thing to pop up in a religious conversation is instrumental music. We're most *noticeably* different from everyone else in that we happen to sing *a cappella.* On that one issue alone, we are definitely on the wrong side of the tracks as far as Protestant Christianity is concerned. (Chapter 13 promises a surprise in that regard.)

Add to this apparent uniqueness a lack of formally-ordained clergy, organizational superstructure, or written creed—not to mention our once-stated insistence on having austere houses of worship—and you find that we've not only been on the other side of the tracks, but we've not even been close enough to feel the rumble of the locomotive when it passes by!

But times change and, as we know, nobody likes to stay on the wrong side of the tracks if he can help it. So, before you can say ten times hurriedly, "We wanna be mainstream," you start seeing congregations whose new buildings have crosses over the baptistries, and steeples on the roofs. There are gymnasiums and kitchens, and, of course, parking lots commensurate in size with the latest church-growth theories pioneered by successful megachurches.

Come Easter or Christmas Sundays, and we're no longer left behind the rest of the world in embarrassing denial. In one quick generation we go from obligatory Christmas-bashing sermons to joyously singing Christmas carols in the worship. (And, "Wouldn't they sound even better with a full orchestra?" some are asking.)

Of course we are not the only ones trying desperately to be mainstream "like the nations around us."[10] (Note, for example, how some of the holiness fellowships have moved from strictly no make-up to Tammy Faye-like excess.) But we have to be honest about our longing for respectability. The desire to conform is very, *very* strong.

The only problem, as we have seen, is that some of the things we are wanting to do these days in order to be more socially upmarket are simply contrary to the biblical pattern. And that's why so many in our fellowship are calling for us to rethink just how committed we want to be to that pattern. If what it means is having to stay anywhere near the tracks we've just crossed, many among us are ready to throw it out.

Hermeneutics—what a troublemaker!

More Surprising Lessons From Jewish Reformers

The tie between social acceptability and calls for "clipping the beard" of biblical authority could be established well enough on home turf, simply by looking at the movement of the churches of Christ from the more conservative rural South, to the more liberal affluent North. Look behind the scenes of the controversial issues within the church over the past two centuries and you'll invariably find that economic and social expectations had already preceded attempts at doctrinal justifications. Sect-to-denomination evolution is always as much, if not more so, a matter of changed group consciousness as it is purely a matter of doctrine.

But looking outside of ourselves may be even more instructive than a re-telling of restorationist history. Take, for example, this insight into the history of Judaism, as provided by Ellis Rivkin in his article on "Some Historical Aspects of Authority in Judaism":

> The problem of authority in these epochs was most crucial when profound historical changes so altered the structure of society that large numbers of Jews challenged the very structure of authority then prevailing.[11]

When faced with the struggle to be less conspicuous in a changing culture, Jewish reformers instinctively knew that they would have to challenge orthodox authority. They realized that they had to have a "new hermeneutic"—less inhibitive, less strict, less *conspicuously different* from the culture in which they found themselves.

When we see what happened to the thinking of these reformist Jews in the wake of radical cultural change, we can see more clearly than ever that what we are facing in our own fellowship is much larger than whether "command, example, and necessary inference" is the best hermeneutic we can come up with in searching out the mind of God. Just look at these uncanny parallels with the Jewish reformers, as insightfully provided by Michael A. Meyer in his *Response to Modernity—A History of the Reform Movement in Judaism.*[12] Insert the "churches of Christ" in the following snippets, and then tell me it doesn't describe our current situation to a "T":

On the effect of culture: "It was not merely a movement for doctrinal or liturgical reform unrelated to the realities of Jewish existence....It was a movement among Jews whose individual and collective motivation transcended the purely religious...."

"Those members of Jewish communities possessing the most contact with the outside world were the more likely to incorporate its values."

On altering doctrine: "Jews in premodern times regarded their religion as eternal and unchanging....   No Jewish leader was permitted *to add to it or to subtract from it* [my emphasis]."

On "New Age"-like thinking: "Before the first practical reforms in the worship service were undertaken, a religious mentality emerged which made it requisite to measure traditions against a new standard located in the subjective consciousness of the individual."

"To the extent that they attributed theological status to the spirit of the new age or to the conscience of the individual, they undermined the exclusive claims of Jewish revelation and created a form of Judaism that was radically new."

On Enlightenment rationalism: "Early as well as later Reformers prided themselves on their rationalism....."

"For a few, the ideas of the French Enlightenment became a substitute faith replacing belief in the revelation at Sinai."

On pluralism: [A more hospitable attitude on the part of some Christians] drew Jews into broader cultural identifications and soon made traditional Judaism seem excessively particularistic and inappropriate in the modern world."

On legalism and a "new hermeneutic": "Their preoccupation with the Bible, not as a legal document but as the spiritual treasure of Judaism, shifted the focus away from the normative authority of Jewish classical texts to their literary qualities and their value for religious exaltation. The newly gained aesthetic sense, first applied to the Bible, would later be focused on the worship service of the synagogue."

On cultural conformity: "Frankel called upon his readers to remove the barriers that separated them from 'sensitive human beings' who were non-Jews and attempt 'to keep pace with the spirit of the times.' Jews should adopt prevalent modes of behavior 'so that the Jewish citizen will not stand out too much from the Christian.'"

No Corner On Cultural Questions

Who ever would guess that Jews a continent and a century removed from us would have struggled over the same issues which now confront our fellowship! Not only are we not unique in facing the challenges of culture, but we are not even unique in facing the challenge of *twentieth-century* or *exclusively-Christian* culture. In whatever century, for Jew and Christian alike, the challenge to biblical authority has always been present. Solomon had it right: There is truly nothing new under the sun.

Whether it be the cultural synagogue or the cultural church, the temptation to "clip our doctrinal beards" in order to appear less conspicuous to the world around us is simply too inviting. Culture's call to pluralism only serves to bring us into closer contact with those whose own hypocritical sense of pluralism does not include acceptance of a God of revelation.

Rubbing elbows with a pluralistic culture will not serve to make us more appreciative of either our characteristic hermeneutic or, more importantly, our distinctive calling in Christ. It will only serve to remind us of how *different* we are and to demonstrate how desperately we feel the need to conform—even, if necessary, at the cost of fundamentally changing our view of the authority of God's written Word.

The more turmoil I see in the religious world beyond the borders of our own fellowship, the more I believe in both pattern hermeneutics and pattern theology. As a *pattern hermeneutic*, "command, example, and necessary inference" is by no means a perfect way of understanding the Bible, but it embodies the right idea. It is confessional and submissive. It honors God's leading. And it fully respects the *pattern theology* in which Christ becomes the standard by which all things are to be judged.

Unfortunately, both our pattern hermeneutic and our pattern theology are under continuous assault from an altogether different kind of pattern. We see it in the loosened underpinnings of Scripture which permits Archbishop Carey's inclusive Anglican theology; in the replacement of Western truth assumptions by Calcutta-like mystical perceptions; in the Church on the Way's unscriptural accommodative move to Saturday worship; in the decline of "Liberal" churches which have quickly and irresponsibly adapted to culture; and in the shocking attempt to radically change sexual ethics in official Presbyterian doctrine. Paul referred to this "pattern" in his letter to the Romans as *the pattern of this world*. Have you ever considered the fact that culture has its own hermeneutic? "Do not conform any longer to the pattern of this world," Paul urges, "but be transformed by the renewing of your mind."[13]

We in the churches of Christ have something very special to share with the world, if only we don't lose it for ourselves first. With the call for a new, more culturally conformist hermeneutic, the real issue is not *whether* pattern, but *which?* Will ours be *the pattern of sound teaching* or *the pattern of this world?*

NINE

Enlightenment Rationality— An Unlikely Bogeyman

This is why Science has so little of a religious tendency; deductions have no power of persuasion....Many a man will live and die upon a dogma; no man will be a martyr for a conclusion.
—John Henry Newman

I must confess that I am completely mystified by a common theme being voiced by those who are calling for a new hermeneutic. On every front, I encounter vicious assaults against seventeenth and eighteenth century "Enlightenment rationality," as if faith and doctrine are somehow victims of reason. In one scholarly (reasoned!) article after another, the old hermeneutic of "command, example, and necessary inference" is sneered at as being the product of the Enlightenment—the Age of Reason.

At this point I feel somewhat like the writer of Hebrews in his plea: "We have much to say about this, but it is hard to explain...."[1] Not many of us have any working knowledge of the seventeenth century or Enlightenment rationality. Philosophy is not what turns most of us on. (In fact, I fear that the very mention of the word will turn some readers off!) But I'm left with no option but to tackle a subject that has been widely dealt with in other books which have recently circulated among our fellowship.

So please bear with me for this one chapter. I've made every effort to cut through the intellectualism that surrounds the discussion, so much so that I run the risk of being charged by the scholars with gross oversimplification. I think you'll be rewarded if you take in some of what's being talked about in our fellowship today, but if it begins to look like too much "scholar fodder," feel free at any point to skip to the next chapter.

Introducing John Locke and Scientific Method

In the current controversy over hermeneutics, Enlightenment philosopher John Locke—not Satan—has seemingly become our greatest enemy! Locke (1632-1704) was a British philosopher whose work spanned religion, politics, education, science, and psychology. A prolific writer, he is best known for his *Essay Concerning Human Understanding, A Letter Concerning Toleration,* and *The Reasonableness of Christianity.*

Locke's most significant contribution to Enlightenment rationalism resulted from his attempt to refute a widely-held belief that when children are born they have imprinted in their minds "the whole of God's truth" from which they gradually deduce rules of morality. By this view, morality was thought to be innate, or inborn.

Of course, it was the age-old *nature* versus *nurture* argument. Are we shaped by our basic nature, or do we develop according to the way we are nurtured? (In a slightly different arena, which is more important, genetics or environment?) If you have seen the classic movie, "Lord of the Flies" (in which the object is to observe how young boys trapped on a deserted island form their notions of morality apart from the influence of culture), you have the basic argument in cinematic black and white.

And what, one might ask, did Paul mean when he said that the Gentiles "do by nature things required by the law" since "the requirements of the law are written on their hearts"?[2] Was he saying that morality and religious faith are natural human traits? If so, why are there so many different world religions?

Asking that very question himself, Locke took the side of *nurture*, saying that children are born with clean slates knowing virtually nothing. Through tutoring by parents and teachers, and by personal experience, children eventually make use of their own gradually-developing powers of reason to discover the rules of morality that are apparent everywhere in nature and revealed more precisely in Scripture.

Interestingly for our fellowship, Locke took much of his argument from the book of Romans, which (like us) he understood to refute the doctrine of original sin. According to Locke, children neither come into the world imprinted with "the whole of God's truth," nor burdened with the sin of Adam. In every way, they come in with a clean slate.

But look what a sharp contrast that made with the kind of thinking that was contemporary to Locke's time. Pre-Enlightenment thinking moved from general assumptions about life—usually theological in nature—to more particular conclusions (the deductive method). Science prior to Copernicus and Galileo, for example, had almost blindly accepted the theory that the earth was the center of the universe. Instead of looking at the available physical evidence, theologians had deduced from the idea of Creation that the planet on which man (God's highest creation) lived simply *had to be* the center of the universe.

By contrast, Locke's thinking moved from particular observations to more abstract ideas and general assumptions (the inductive method). And with that, the modern era of scientific method was born. Scientific method using inductive reasoning was a revolutionary way of thinking, albeit consistent with the achievements of seventeenth century science itself, through which the world had finally come to know that the earth revolved around the sun, and not vice versa.

Back to Hermeneutics

What does all this have to do with hermeneutics? Restorationist Alexander Campbell is said to have been so enamored with Locke's method of analysis that he adopted it as a sure-fire method of understanding the Bible—a method which has been handed down to those of us in the tradition of the churches of Christ. "The Bible is a book of facts," Campbell insisted, "not of opinions, theories, abstract generalities, nor of verbal definitions. It is a book of awful fact, grand and sublime beyond description...."[3]

For many people in the church today, that view of Scripture has become offensive. To their thinking, it robs Scripture of its mystery and reduces man's quest for God to the rigidity of a scientific formula. But Campbell's call for a "divine science of religion" must be taken in its historical context. What Campbell was confronting in his day (much like Locke himself) was a travesty of burdensome church tradition and bitter denominational schism resulting from centuries of abuse in which basic biblical teaching had largely been ignored.

Campbell's fascination with inductive reasoning was its potential for getting back to the unadulterated simplicity of the Bible. For Campbell, there was no allure in knowing biblical facts merely for facts' sake. He wasn't playing Trivial Pursuit—not even the Bible version! For him, it was a matter of biblical facts as opposed to *human opinion*. Divinely inspired facts in contrast to *speculative theories*. First century facts in their superiority over the embellishment of *church tradition*. Should we ever want it otherwise?

Nor should we be thrown off track by Campbell's use of the word "facts." To us, *facts* has a rather clinical ring—hardly worthy of the great truths of the gospel. But look again at what Campbell said: the Bible is a book of "awful fact"—meaning *awe-inspiring, full of awe,* and *awesome!* Biblical facts, he reminds us, are "*grand* and *sublime beyond description.*"

It is important to understand that Campbell's "facts" were not merely historical dates, names, and places. True enough, the *Acts* of the Apostles could well have been named the *Facts* of the Apostles. But even Luke's historical record of the early church goes out of its way to bring home the fact of sin and the fact of salvation; the fact of Jesus' messiahship and the fact of his lordship. For Campbell, you can be sure, it was the scandalous fact of the cross, the actual fact of Christ's burial, and the all-significant literal fact of his resurrection that formed the bedrock of the Christian system.

I wish that all I was hearing among our fellowship was the obvious: that "facts" which appeal only to the raw intellect have little impact on how we live or who we are becoming. Clearly, Jesus himself dealt with more than the mind. Indeed, certain aspects of his ministry—the parables, the miracles, the cross—are intended to *go around reason* in order to first strike the heart. Purely rational "facts" cannot be the soil which gives rise to the whole of man: emotion, imagination, behavior, personality, and relationships—as well as intellect.

Unfortunately, today's assault against "facts" is most often tied to the very matters which touch on the intellect—namely, doctrine. If facts aren't appropriate to doctrine, what is?

Admittedly, any hermeneutic runs the risk of being treated as a mathematical formula or scientific equation in which a scripture here (taken out of context) and a scripture there (not exactly on point) could be offered as some well-developed matter of doctrine. But I'm impressed by the fact that among those who first passed on the roots of our particular hermeneutic were scholars of the highest caliber, well-versed in historical, literary, and theological contexts. Clearly, they were making no mad dashes to doctrine, whether or not they actually got it right. (And, naturally, sometimes they *didn't* get it right.)

Nor do they deserve having laid at their feet the popular charge that a reasoned hermeneutic somehow prevents heart-felt Christianity. Their search for doctrinal truth did not leave them unconcerned about emotion, imagination, behavior, personality, and relationships. Today's critics need to do some serious soul-searching as to which era has produced the better spiritual product. Surely, we kid ourselves if we think that the church in the 90's is more spiritually vibrant than the church of the "old hermeneutic" fifty years ago. Even given the many moral and cultural changes that might have an impact on that comparison, at the very least one can be sure that "the old hermeneutic" has not been a hindrance to the humble godliness displayed by our predecessors in the faith.

Uncommon Common Sense

At issue is whether there is such a thing as an *objective pattern* from which faith and doctrine can be derived, especially by the average Bible reader using his or her own common sense. Scan today's scholarly discussion of biblical hermeneutics and you'll see a great deal of elitist disdain for common sense, as if its use somehow elevates human logic over divine revelation.

However, unless God intended the Bible only for scholars, he must have revealed himself in such a way that the ordinary man and woman could use his or her common sense to understand the sacred text. As John Locke put it in his *Reasonableness of Christianity*, the New Testament is "a collection of writings, designed by God for the instruction of the illiterate bulk of mankind...."[4] Naturally, that never meant discarding history or context or grammar or any other factor that might shed light on one's "common sense" understanding. But, by design, it was a revelation which could be read, evaluated, and interpreted by any ordinary person committed to diligent study.

Through such a revelation, even the incomprehensible becomes comprehensible. As Paul wrote to the Ephesians, "I pray that you, being rooted and established in love, may have power, together with all the saints, to grasp how wide and long and high and deep is the love of Christ, and to know this love that surpasses knowledge—that you may be filled to the measure of all the fullness of God."[5]

An appeal to the use of "common sense" was never intended to replace an appeal to the heart. For example, in his Ephesian letter, Paul prays that "the eyes of your heart may be enlightened in order that you may know the hope to which he has called you."[6] But, lest anyone think that the "grasping" to which Paul refers in the earlier passage is something that takes place wholly apart from Scripture, the context suggests otherwise. Only a few sentences earlier, Paul praised God for having chosen him as a servant to "preach to the Gentiles the unsearchable riches of Christ, and *to make plain to everyone* the administration of this mystery."[7]

For those who seek mystery beyond the factually mundane, surely the process of divine revelation—a God who exists beyond all human logic and words actually communicating with man—should be mystery enough!

And even within that revelation is ample mystery to keep all of us humble. Rationalist that he was, John Locke agreed. "I wish I could say there were no mysteries in it; I acknowledge there are to me, and I fear always will be."[8] In his *Essay Concerning Human Understanding*, Locke used scriptural language to underscore the mystery within revelation, reminding us that it contains "such Things, as Eye hath not seen, nor Ear heard, nor hath it entered into the Heart of Man to conceive."[9]

To be sure, common sense must not be a license for *non*-sense. If the much-caricatured old farmer saying "It says what it means and means what it says!" is still around, I'd be surprised if he has enough common sense to come in out of the rain. Anyone truly using common sense will know that "the unsearchable riches of Christ" is indeed holy ground, to be approached only with the utmost wonder and respect. Common sense will never fully appreciate "love that surpasses knowledge," but it *can* comprehend both the reality of the love itself and the rapturous thought that Christ's love for us is beyond all understanding.

The alternatives to a common sense understanding of the Bible are too scary to contemplate. The first alternative is a rather academic (scientific?) historical approach which too often puts the average Bible reader at the mercy of biblical scholars sitting in detached aloofness in the ivory towers of universities. Sadly, scholarly criticism has too often tended toward skepticism. With enormous respect for my colleagues in our own church-related universities, I think they too would agree that institutions of higher learning are not notorious for being centers of great personal faith.

The more likely, and even scarier, alternative is an "anti-sense" approach to Scripture, wherein there is a subjective, mystical reading of the text. Discarding the more obvious "common sense" meaning of a passage, the subjective "anti-sense" approach risks coming away from Scripture with nothing but "non-sense."

If our basic approach to Scripture has seemed overly simplistic, nevertheless it has the advantage of being "community property." Through it, the Bible belongs to the plumber, housewife, electrician, and astronaut as well as to the Greek scholar and professor of religion. Not that the ivory tower has no gift to share, no caution to enjoin on those who insist on using our hermeneutic for mad dashes to doctrine.

The irony is that the scholars themselves use inductive reasoning in reaching their "more learned" conclusions about the historical and literary roots of Scripture. In fact, it is also inductive reasoning that leads so many today to reach the conclusion that the "old hermeneutic" has outlived its usefulness. Instance after instance of scriptural abuse is cited in support of the death sentence for "command, example, and necessary inference." And that is inductive reasoning!

We're Not Talking About a Mathematical Formula

I would like to think that our current controversy is one of semantics, in which we are discussing two different issues without recognizing a distinction about which we fundamentally might agree. Probably all of us could agree, for instance, that "command, example, and necessary inference" should never be considered a computer program which, used as a scanning device over the entire data base of Scripture, could automatically compute a Christ-centered theology. If *that* is what its critics mean by rationalistic scientific method, then, of course, they are right.

However, there is a certain unfairness in this "straw man" argument. I personally know of no one who has ever made that claim on behalf of our hermeneutic. Certainly it was not a claim generally made by those who initially articulated our hermeneutic.

What's more, our hermeneutic doesn't deserve the popular charge that it is nothing more than a Locke-inspired syllogism. Just look at these words by John W. Yolton, Dean of Rutgers College, who is recognized as the world's leading authority on John Locke:

> This specification of the meaning of "reason"
> occurs in a chapter in which Locke attacks the

traditional notion of formal, syllogistic reasoning. Reason as a faculty of the mind is not dependent upon syllogisms and rules for deriving conclusions from premises. These are *artificial* aids to that faculty. Locke stresses the *naturalness* of this faculty. It is given to all of us by God for our use; we have an obligation to use it and to use it well.[10]

Far from promoting a clinical, mathematical, formula-like approach to hermeneutics, Locke actually urged the very type of textually-based Bible study being called for today by many in the "new hermeneutics" movement. Writing about Paul's epistles, Locke said that to understand an author requires us to "understand his terms, in the sense he uses them, and not as they are appropriated, by each man's particular philosophy, to conceptions that never entered the mind" of that author. Using the author's own words, we should "paint his very ideas and thoughts in our minds."[11]

Locke insisted on having information about the "occasion of his writing" and the "temper and circumstances" of the people for whom he wrote. He wanted to get some sense of the author himself, his experiences, his attitudes and values. Does this sound anything like the kind of rigid scientific method of which Locke and Campbell have lately been accused?

And here is where I return to my absolute dumbfoundedness over the association between the "old hermeneutic" and Enlightenment thinking. Something very strange is going on here—something very much akin to the pot calling the kettle black. But in order to see the astounding contradictions of our current controversy, we must take one more brief detour back through history.

Second Generation Rationalists

Those who followed after John Locke in the Enlightenment ("Lockeans," if you will) were as different from John Locke as some of the so-called "Campbellites" were from Alexander Campbell. (Actually, "Lockeans" were *far more different!*) The revelation-affirming, Christ-believing,

Judgment-fearing Locke could not have been more distant from the next generation of rationalists, who took what Locke said about the importance of reason in the search for Truth and turned it into the elevation of human reason in the pursuit of self-will. (I wouldn't be surprised if there are some scholars in our own fellowship who can identify with Locke in having seen their students take what they taught about this very topic and shape it into something they would never condone.)

Less devout minds in the 18th century based an entirely secular philosophy on Locke's Christian-oriented ideas of human understanding. As the saying goes, Locke would have turned over in his grave to learn of his unwitting impact on the history of religious belief (rather, disbelief) in Western Europe.

How did it happen? Partly because Locke often went overboard in his zealous defense of reason as against rigid church tradition, frothy emotionalism, and fanciful interpretations of Scripture—all common in his day. Reaction always tends toward extremism. (A caution to some of us, perhaps?)

Even today, Locke's philosophy is in the eye of the beholder. I confess that my own initial foray into Locke's thinking went entirely askew because of a book on Locke which was obviously written by a non-believer. Focusing through purely secular lenses on Locke's more extreme statements, the author arrived at conclusions totally at odds with the kind of faith Locke actually espoused. Other books, written by men of faith, depict Locke as the true believer he was. It's not difficult to see, then, how easily Locke might have been misinterpreted by those who came after him.

Second-generation rationalism was also undoubtedly influenced by Locke's minimalist view of the New Testament. He believed the church had no business maintaining any doctrines other than those which pertained to salvation, namely belief in Jesus as Messiah and repentance as shown through a lifetime of virtuous works. He was so opposed to *traditional* church doctrine that he came close to rejecting *any* doctrine pertaining to the church.

(Is not this same minimalist view of the New Testament a familiar feature of the cultural church's call for a new hermeneutic? More to the point, look how different Locke and Campbell were in this one respect. Critics of Campbell's methodology complain of his overemphasis on the Epistles and "church-related" doctrine. No one would ever have accused John Locke of such an emphasis. On at least this one point, Locke and most of those who call for a new hermeneutic would fit comfortably on the same pew.)

Unlike Locke, his disciples in the age of Enlightenment assumed that through inductive reasoning they could find God on their own. Unlike Locke, they didn't need any revealed Scripture to provide a framework for their rational thinking. And where Locke had proper disdain for church tradition when it contradicted the plain teaching of Scripture, Locke's disciples simply chucked the whole bit—church, doctrine, faith, and even a personal God.

(Of course, it didn't help any that the official Church had fostered centuries of scientific ignorance by perpetuating faulty deductions from biblically-based truths—yet another caution to those of us today who take a more conservative view of Scripture. Are we making *faulty use* of the "old hermeneutic" in any way that might be driving others into the arms of the cultural church?)

Enlightenment rationalists were not necessarily atheists. Many became Deists, believing in a God who, as Creator, had given man the power to reason. Their God created the universe and mankind, then immediately went into retirement. The best ongoing position that God could claim was a rather ill-defined "benevolent Providence." Man was left alone to discover and achieve through his own reason. In the age of Enlightenment, reason became enthroned and God took a back seat.

Curiously enough, Enlightenment rationalism, as later reflected in the writings of our own Founding Fathers, became the very bedrock of our nation's link to God. It was that fiercely deistic and rationalistic Thomas Jefferson who penned the Declaration of Independence, with its sublime references to "self-evident truths" and to "the Creator" from whom our inalienable rights derive. (John Locke had first articulated the concepts.) And it was Thomas Paine, author of the rationalistic *Age of Reason*, who helped pave the way for the religious liberty we now enjoy.

Enlightenment rationality has always been "good news-bad news." The zealous quest for rationally-pursued knowledge is by no means the worst enemy Christian belief has ever faced. To the contrary, it was Enlightenment rationalists who laid the foundation for a nation which would become known, not as a *deist* nation, but as a *Christian* nation. Sadly, of course, neither Jefferson nor Paine ever personally accepted biblical authority in the realm of religion, or the Bible as revealed from God, or even a God working directly in the affairs of men and nations.

Hermeneutics and Hypocrisy

Back on track, here now is where pots and kettles have begun doing some strange finger-pointing lately. What irony that a hermeneutic honoring the authority of revealed Scripture (and, more importantly, the God who gave it to us as our guide to him) should be castigated as the product of Enlightenment thinking! At the very heart of Enlightenment thinking (following Locke) was the belief that no divine revelation was needed in order to find truth. It was thought that the mind alone—through its God-given gift of reason—could fully comprehend the universe and answer the needs of humankind.

For those in the cultural church who clamor for a new hermeneutic in order to get around the plain meaning of Scripture, the Enlightenment's move away from the authority of Scripture made it the "new hermeneutic" movement of its day!

The only difference is that Enlightenment rationalism was up front and honest about its elevation of human reason over divine revelation, while the cultural church's "new hermeneutic" mentality kids itself into thinking that it is too spiritual for such pride. The truth is that our own rationally-applied, but biblically-centered, hermeneutic was intended as an expression of humility in the leading of God's Word, while, for those caught up in the cultural church, a new hermeneutic means nothing more than elevating culture (Man) over doctrine (God).

Enlightenment Thinking—Rational or Intuitive?

Contrary to the rumor, it is the cultural church's "new hermeneutic" mentality, not the "old hermeneutic," which is most representative of Enlightenment thinking. For example, without any sacred scriptures of its own, the Enlightenment's unofficial religion, Deism, was always a matter of *individual judgment*. For Deists, there was only an undefined God whom each person could discern for himself. Likewise, the cultural church's call for a new hermeneutic is all about the abandonment of an *objective*, universally-instructive biblical authority and the acceptance of a more *subjective*, personal leading of the Scriptures.

The Enlightenment's hatred of church doctrine for getting in the way of one's own subjective reason was not unlike the cultural church's barely disguised distrust of any systematic doctrinal pursuit. Whether for Enlightenment rationalists or for today's culturalists, revealed doctrine has always been the archenemy of those who pursue their own brand of self-determination.

In an assault on the certainty of doctrine, there are some among us (fortunately, only a few so far) who are calling for a new hermeneutic which is closely aligned with the Enlightenment's insistence that reason (even to the exclusion of Scripture) is the only reliable religious truth. One particular statement of John Locke needs careful scrutiny in this regard. "No proposition," said Locke, "can be received for divine revelation or obtain the assent due to all such, if it be contradictory to our clear intuitive knowledge. Reason must be our last judge and guide in everything."[12]

Taken out of context, it might appear that Locke elevates reason over revelation. What he was really saying is closer to the thought: "Discern the spirits." In today's terms, he was simply describing what we ourselves do when, by the use of reason, we reject the Koran and the Book of Mormon as divine revelation and accept only the Bible as God's Word.

Unfortunately, Locke's disciples missed the point and did in fact end up elevating reason over revelation. Unfortunately, too, they got caught in the inevitable trap that always surfaces when God's revelation is replaced by man's reason. Look once again at what preceded Locke's reference to "reason:" "No proposition," said Locke, "can be received for divine revelation or obtain the assent due to all such, if it be contradictory to our clear *intuitive* knowledge." It's easy to concentrate on the word "reason" and miss the true thrust of what the second-generation rationalists were all about. Move the spotlight to the word *intuitive*, and you'll understand the mindset of Locke's followers. Their idea of reason had more to do with "intuition" than "true knowledge."

That's *intuitive*, as in *my* reason and *your* reason regarding what is religiously acceptable. That's *intuitive*, as in whatever *feels* right. That's *intuitive*, as in whatever answers the call of current culture. For the Enlightenment rationalists, reason became but a masquerade for self-will.

One must realize how important it is that we see what was really going on behind the scenes in the Enlightenment, and what even now can subtly sabotage more noble calls for a new hermeneutic. Both then and now, "reason" is capable of posing as a supremely deceptive front for subjective, intuitive, "feel good" self-determination.

In the cultural church's call for a new hermeneutic, the story is the same, but with a sinister twist. The story is still one of dethroning reasonably understood revelation and replacing it with individual subjectivity. The sinister twist is that the "old hermeneutic" is being vilified as the product of Enlightenment rationality, when what it does best is to elevate the objective truth of divine revelation over the subjectivity of human reason! (To the extent that human reason is obviously involved in the making of "inferences," that part of our hermeneutic warrants extreme caution. As Thomas Campbell warned, inferences must be drawn only with strict faithfulness to scriptural guidelines.)

It is not the rational approach of the "old hermeneutic" that we should fear, but rather the kind of intuitive self-will by which all things—including God's revelation—are judged. Therein lay the hidden idolatry of Enlightenment rationalism. And therein lies the disguised idolatry of any "new hermeneutic" which allows us to replace the authority of Scripture with our own intuitive idea about what is right and wrong for the church at the end of the twentieth century.

Undermining Scripture by Cultural Irrelevance

Even the Enlightenment's method of discounting Christian doctrine is mimicked in the rush for a new hermeneutic. In much the same way that Deists renounced divine revelation as "groundless *historical* confusion," many of today's advocates for a new hermeneutic would have us believe that, as far as the twentieth century is concerned, first century teaching is also "groundless *cultural* confusion." "How could we possibly be bound by antiquated rules no longer suitable for the tenor of the times?" we are asked. Perhaps the questions should run the other way: Are today's culturalists embarrassed by any scripture which dares to be counter-culture? (A woman not permitted to *teach*?) Does the "old hermeneutic" seem abysmally unenlightened?

It is here—right here—where those who seek less rationalistic doctrine and more Spirit-led faith must put that commitment to the test. For it is precisely at the point where human logic rebels that faith in God's leading must come to the fore. To the Jews who demanded miraculous signs and to the Greeks who looked for intellectual explanations, Paul preached only the stumblingblock and foolishness of Christ crucified.[13] For most of his hearers, Paul's message made absolutely no sense. It was neither what they expected, nor what they wanted.

When society's standards and expectations come into conflict with clear biblical teaching, it's not just a matter of maintaining blind rationalistic legalism. It's a matter of reaching out in faith to believe that God often deals in the unlikely, the unpopular, and even the unthinkable.

Is the call for a new hermeneutic a noble quest for rising above purely-intellectual rationalism (as it is for some), or is it (for others) the cheapest rationalism of all—the kind which pays lip service to biblical authority but rejects the plain teaching of God's Word whenever it happens not to ratify our own notions of justice and fair play?

For Enlightenment rationalists, Deists, and today's culture-captive Christian, something which most of us do too often—that is, rationalizing away any given scripture which is felt to be "distasteful"—has been raised to an art form. That in a nutshell is the true spirit of the Enlightenment. No "new hermeneutic" is likely to rid any of us completely of that temptation, and—given the current cultural assault against scriptural authority—is even more likely to open the door and invite it right in.

TEN

Narrative, Myth, And Metaphor

A Scotch woman said to her minister, "I love to hear you preach. You get so many things out of your text that aren't really there."
—Watchman-Examiner

Some today are suggesting what is called a "narrative hermeneutic." They are taking their lead from such people as Walter Fisher, whose book, *Human Communication as Narration: Toward a Philosophy of Reason, Value, and Action*,[1] proposes the use of "story-telling" as a life-changing way of understanding authoritative texts. In pursuit of a more spiritual alternative to tired hermeneutical formula, "narrative hermeneutics" is being offered as a way to keep the Bible alive through "story."

It is important to note that their understanding of narrative as "story" does not mean *fictional* story, but *divine* story. For them, it is more like what we often sing in the familiar song, "Tell me the old, old story."

"Narrative theology" (in contrast to "narrative hermeneutics") is about getting to the reality behind "book, chapter, and verse." It's the cop on the beat asking, "Okay, you guys, what's the story here? What's *really* going on?" It's seeing baptism, not as the fifth step in a formulistic "five steps to salvation," but as a faith-responsive re-enactment of Christ's own sublime story of death, burial, and resurrection. It's context. It's meat. It's substance. It's true meaning!

And for all those reasons, "narrative theology" deserves careful consideration. What is the Bible, after all, but *story?* From the story of Creation in the opening pages of Genesis to the story of the final culmination of all things in the Revelation, the Bible is a book of stories. Who among us was not weaned on the stories of Moses, Joseph, and David from our favorite "Children's Bible Stories" book?

If credentials are important in the area of appreciating narrative, mine should be impeccable. It was my idea for the chronological arrangement of the NIV to be called *The Narrated Bible.* I wanted the entire collection of biblical stories to be presented as the single divine drama that it is, so that we might not miss *the whole story* of God interacting with man throughout history. Over the past several years, I have crisscrossed the nation pleading for the Bible not to be simply *studied* in bits and pieces, but *read* in its wholeness—from cover to cover.

The very impetus behind a chronological arrangement is to facilitate the telling of the story—in the order that it actually happened, with present-tense commentary along the way to enhance *personal involvement* in the story. It's a story, not simply to be read, but *experienced!* Perhaps more than most, I believe in the importance of narrative. I believe in the importance of story.

Green Light, Yellow Light

But what about a "narrative *hermeneutic?*" Despite my appreciation for the divine narrative, I am compelled to say that the idea of a "narrative hermeneutic" warrants caution— *great* caution! In truth, I would think there should be expressions of concern coming from both sides of the fence. Have those who are calling for a new hermeneutic realized how terribly dependent "narrative hermeneutics" is on *inference?* The point of "stories" must always be inferred! If "necessary inference" is really the danger it is seen to be, we are forced to use it all the more when viewing Scripture as narrative.

Our first problem, of course, is knowing what will happen if anyone gets the idea that obvious propositional biblical statements are to be viewed solely or even primarily as *metaphors*—those little "mini-stories" which, whether as a single word or a complete paragraph, can pack such a wallop because of their vivid comparative images. (For example, baptism, as "death, burial, and resurrection." Or, the Lord's Supper as "body" and "blood.")

In point of fact, some scholars today are insisting that *all* discourse is essentially metaphoric. But if that is the case, how are we to evaluate such propositional statements as Jesus' own words, "My command is this: Love each other as I have loved you"?[2] Or, his singularly bold claim, "I am the way and the truth and the life. No one comes to the Father except through me"?[3] Is Jesus' claim to be taken at face value, or simply interpreted metaphorically as a "meaningful story"?

To take another example, it is certainly true that the laws of Moses were part of a covenant story about God and the nation of Israel, but they were *laws* nevertheless. Not poetry, not parable, not metaphor. Transforming *laws* into *metaphor* would be as violative of the text as transforming poetry into statutes.

We must learn to honor the integrity of each part of Scripture. If God had meant for all of Scripture to be taken as metaphor, surely he wouldn't have included specific rules and regulations. If he had meant for all of Scripture to be "commands," why would he have given us the beauty of poetry?

Those who have suggested a "narrative hermeneutic" have themselves been quick to point out how we have abused even metaphor by concentrating, for example, almost exclusively on the metaphor of *church* as *kingdom*, rather than on the metaphor of *Christ* as *King*. (Which only serves to remind us that *no* hermeneutic is a magic wand. One, two, three, they all fall down!)

Just as with a more systematic hermeneutic like "command, example, and necessary inference," *narrative, metaphor*, and *story* have built-in risks. The first and most obvious is that not everyone will appreciate the difference between the story of King David and the story of King Arthur. The problem is that, when most people use the word *story*, more often than not they are thinking of a *fictional* story. At a minimum, it is a story told by man. No matter how hard we might try to make the distinction, there will always be those who will miss the idea completely.

Walter Fisher is no help in this regard. He sees us humans as *Homo narrans,* "story-telling animals." When it comes to revelation, the Bible sees it in an entirely different way, with *Deus narrans,* a "story-telling *God!* Not only is the Bible not fiction, but it is not simply a *man*-told story. It is a *God*-told story!

Yes, *you* know that, and *I* know that, but will another generation raised on a "narrative hermeneutic" know that? That "other generation," it should be noted, is already convinced that today's philosophers are right in referring to us as "animals," if only of a higher order because of our supposedly evolved capacity for story-telling. The idea of divine revelation to God-made man already suffers from the evolutionary belief that man is not really God-made, and is therefore free to make up his own stories.

Given that premise, it is easy to see why, for many people, one story is as good as another. As Fisher himself suggests, people will decide which story is right *for them,* depending upon whether or not a given story "rings true" as compared with their own life experiences.

Again, maybe you and I can rise above our own subjectivity to acknowledge the objective truth of, say, Christ's exclusive claims: "I am *the* way; *the* truth; and *the* life." But how can we be sure that everyone else will follow suit?

The sad fact is that, for all of us, the *world's* story has a nasty habit of at least *sounding like* it is true. ("How can there possibly be *only one* way of looking at life? *Only one* truth about reality? *Only one* source of life?") In today's culture, each person is guaranteed the right to live his or her own story. And while we might say over and over again that the Bible is not a matter of "my story" vs. "your story," the problem is that, from other people's perspective, that's just *our* story!

How, incidentally, are we to decide which story is ours? According to Fisher, it is through our *rational* capacity, following what we *perceive to be the right story!* Isn't that interesting? Take off the fancy mask and "narrative hermeneutics" claims the same "rationalistic" Enlightenment mentality that has been unduly attributed as the father of the much-maligned "old hermeneutic," while it is in fact the very "intuitive, subjective" mentality behind the cultural church's call for a new hermeneutic!

For anyone who might wish it to be so, "narrative hermeneutics" can be just another method of understanding the Bible which elevates human reason in a process of subjectively deciding what narrative is important and what narrative is not.

"Narrative" As a Relative Hermeneutic

Perhaps the most subtle danger of subjectively viewing the biblical text is not the matter of deciding *which* narrative is important, but the reading of all narrative through different-colored lenses. Whatever our hermeneutic, it will always be true that we will see particular passages in light of the particular presuppositions we bring to the "story." Unfortunately, narrative interpretation gives even more latitude than usual to our primary assumptions.

One quick illustration might be helpful. It's simple enough for us to say that "Jesus was the Messiah," since most of us would agree as to what that means. But there are many people out there who would ask whether Jesus was Messiah *in historical fact*, or simply *thought of himself* as Messiah? How we answer that question will determine how we interpret all the scriptures which tell us about Jesus. With "narrative hermeneutics," we can all be saying the exact same thing, but still have our own, radically different "stories."

Merely mention the possibility that "narrative hermeneutics" might therefore involve an element of relativism and you find a great deal of understandable defensiveness on the part of those whose own attitude toward Scripture is more noble. Yet there is more than one kind of relativism. "My story" vs. "your story" is (typically) the kind of *moral* relativism that rejects the Bible altogether. ("Believe it if you want, but it's not *my* story! It doesn't ring true to me.") It is not this form of relativism that I worry about among the proponents of a "narrative hermeneutic."

Another kind of relativism is more subtle, and thus even more pernicious. It is *cultural* relativism. It's "their story" vs.

"our story," as in *first-century story* but not *twentieth-century story.* Instead of rejecting the Bible altogether, we simply find a way to sidestep it. It's not the story *for our time.* It's this kind of relativism, for example, that prompts current thinking on the changing role of women in the corporate worship of the church.

For Fisher, "The world...is a set of stories that must be chosen among in order for us to live life in a process of continual re-creation." That's longhand for "situation ethics," verifying *God's* (ancient) story by what "rings true" from *our* (modern) story. In approaching the Bible as "their story" vs. "our story," we come very close to "situation ethics," re-creating only what happens to suit our situation.

Many have suggested that we have no major problems when it comes to *exegesis* (discovering what the first-century story was all about for those who experienced it). The problem comes, they say, in making the New Testament story come alive for us today in the same way. Therefore, it is important to ask, not what the story *meant* (for them), but what it *means* (for us).

If you want it in a nutshell, what the hermeneutic controversy is mostly about is whether there should even be a difference between the two—what the Bible meant then and what the Bible means now. The "old hermeneutic" response is that there should be as little difference as possible between their story and ours. Since careful exegesis assures us that "their" story was "His" story, we believe that "their" story is a better test of what is true than is "ours."

The "new hermeneutic" response is that our stories are simply too different to expect much more than a metaphorical connection. Accordingly, it is thought that "command, example, and necessary inference" mixes "their story" and "our story" in unholy union and gets in the way of a more meaningful, more powerful use of biblical metaphor.

Supposedly, the safeguard we have that our current story is still God's story is the leading of the Holy Spirit. (In Chapter 12, we will discuss the role of the Holy Spirit at more length.) It is here, of course—as well as in the fundamental authority of Scripture itself—that "narrative hermeneutics" parts company in a big way from such philosophers as Walter Fisher. The work of the Holy Spirit couldn't be further removed from the cave where we find those first mythical tales being told by *Homo narrans.*

Good, But Not Good Enough

Suppose for a moment that none of the "scary bad" things we've talked about actually result from adoption of a "narrative hermeneutic." Suppose no one thinks of Bible stories as fiction; or makes their own personal experiences the test of biblical authenticity; or treats explicit rules and regulations as mere metaphor. If we could keep all that in check, then, as suggested earlier, there is much to commend a retelling of the "old, old story" in its non-formulistic fullness.

Even so, what remains is the fact that a "narrative hermeneutic" may be *good*, but not always *good enough.* It is *good*, for example, to use the story of Christ's death, burial, and resurrection, in order to see baptism in a more meaningful light; and *good* to be reminded of the story of the cross in our own retelling of it when we participate in the Lord's Supper. But that may not be *good enough*, at least when it comes to questions of practical implementation.

Even when the central story of Christ is retold in the Lord's Supper, what is there in the story of the cross that tells us (as one advocate of "narrative hermeneutics" put it) that "we should do this *every* Sunday when we meet as a believing community"? Or even that we should do it *on Sunday*? Is there something about "story" or "metaphor" that would help us with those very practical questions? Or does it simply not matter about *when* and *how often*?

We face a similar problem with baptism. I hope that my book on baptism, presenting it as the "believer's wedding ceremony," is sufficient evidence of my abhorrence of a ritualistic approach to baptism. But I have to ask what we would know about baptism if all we knew was its metaphorical significance? If metaphor is to be our controlling hermeneutic, we might consider immersion important (*burial* being the metaphor), or we might equally conclude that sprinkling is itself a metaphorical *act* linking up, through the eye of faith, with the metaphorical *story*. (Isn't that exactly the view of those who sprinkle or pour instead of immersing?)

And what in the story of baptism alone would rule out infant baptism? In the absence of biblical example (wherein those who were baptized were always believing adults), the "baptism story" can be (and is) appropriated metaphorically by other fellowships in declaring forgiveness of sins from the earliest days of one's life.

How else did these fellowships ever get to the point of practicing infant baptism except by seeing baptism as a metaphorical re-enactment of the divine story, while ignoring the authoritativeness of New Testament example? If they got the *metaphor*, they missed the *method*. The truth is, of course, that in missing the authorized method they have also missed the richness of the story (calling for a *personal* faith identity with Christ)—with disastrous results!

"Narrative hermeneutics" is *good* for those who see nothing but rule and regulation. But for those who see only metaphor, it will never be *good enough*. It simply isn't designed to "cover all the bases."

The problem for most of us is that we tend to seek one hermeneutic that fits all. To their credit, those who call for a "narrative hermeneutic" acknowledge that it cannot be applied across the board to every type of biblical text. What they do not do, as far as I can tell, is to help us know how to proceed when the "narrative hermeneutic" runs out of room in which to operate. If it can help us better appreciate baptism and the Lord's Supper, what are we left with when we encounter passages which, on their face, are not simply "story," but specifically directive?

If "narrative hermeneutics" is helpful in applying the metaphor of *Christ* as *King*, how are we to approach those passages which clearly refer to the work and organization of the *church* as *kingdom*? Granted that proper narrative thinking would elevate even our idea of *kingdom* (from *organization* to *organism*, for example), we are still left with specific apostolic instruction regarding the qualification of elders, the respective roles of men and women, church discipline, benevolence, orderliness of worship, marriage and divorce, and so on.

If "command, example, and necessary inference" too often disappoints us in getting to the real story about Christ and our relationship with God, "narrative hermeneutics" applied to directive discourse is a disaster waiting to happen. It will never be able to provide us the practical answers that we need in understanding what is to be our day-to-day work and worship before God. Perhaps a "narrative hermeneutic" could help us toward more Christ-centered *faith*, but it could never be the wrench that helps us get a handle on the nuts and bolts of Christian *practice*.

I wish there were evidence of a thoughtful hermeneutical balance in the church today. Unfortunately, it appears that there has been a pendulum swing away from exclusive use of the "old hermeneutic" (even when it is of dubious help when applied to text better understood as "story") to exclusive use of a "narrative-type hermeneutic" (despite the fact that it would be inappropriately applied to text obviously intended to be directive).

Lessons From Islamic Hermeneutics

While waiting for a doctor's appointment recently over in England, I happened across a book from the library in the doctor's home where he did his consultation. The book was titled *Islam and Christian Theology*, by J. Windrow Sweetman. As I leafed through the book, one section immediately caught my attention. It was a section called, "The Method of Interpretation: Exegesis and Philosophy" in which the author analyzed centuries of fierce Islamic debate over proper hermeneutics in the interpretation and application of the Qur'an. Skimming it quickly, I could hardly believe my eyes. It was as if I were reading an article on the "hermeneutics question" right out of the latest edition of *Restoration Quarterly*! It was yet another reminder that ours is not the only hermeneutics struggle. More than that, it focused directly on the idea of *narrative and metaphor*.

Just listen to this: "As a Muslim commentator has said, 'In the Qur'an there is no definition by genus and species [neat doctrinal lists?]; argument is conducted by parable and analogical comparison [narrative?]. If the logician thinks parable is not sufficient, let him think so, because the fundamental test of logic is not necessarily the formal logic of the Greeks but by the way in which a sound mind acts.'"[4]

As Sweetman continues (with my emphases), "This is also the argument of many who support [certain conservative scholars which he names]. *'Back to the Qur'an'* has much backing today in Islam and *common sense* in the interpretation of its rhetorical and imaginative way of presentation."[5]

Can you believe this! "*Back to the Qur'an?*" And *common sense interpretation?* You mean there are also restorationist Muslims? (Not necessarily to be confused with Muslim fundamentalists.)

The answer is definitely yes, and apparently with good reason. For among Islamic scholars had come the introduction of a method of interpreting the Qur'an known as *ta'wil,* which Professor Sweetman defines as "the stretching of the meaning of an expression from its real to its metaphorical sense." Use of the *ta'wil* had increased out of reaction to what some scholars considered to be too much emphasis on the literal meaning of the text and to (of all things) a fear of creeping *rationalism!*

"One great evil was that while Muslims remained ignorant of the rational sciences, they continued ignorant of logical method; but since outside Islam there had arisen a taste for rationalizing, Muslims had formed a taste for the rejection of it, and this had made them lose sight of the fact that Quranic doctrine could be expressed in logical form."

In other words, the scholars had swung like a pendulum from the perceived evil of literalist legalism to the questionable pursuit of their own metaphorical interpretation of the text.

These scholars "maintained that under the literal sense of the Qur'an lay an esoteric meaning. 'The Qur'an is the husk and wisdom-philosophy is the kernel.'"

There was a catch, of course, to this new metaphorical hermeneutic. "Everyone who had the urge to use this method must at least have the status of a *mujtahid,* which one may consider to mean here a person who has the ability to make original research."

The common sense of the ordinary man or woman would not be enough. "It was [a particular scholar's] firm conviction that the masses should be restrained from exegesis which was beyond their powers." This elitist theology, therefore, became the exclusive domain of Islam's equivalent of our own Bible scholars! But it is important to note that, in time, such elitist theology backfired. "They had used *ta'wil* to such an extent and so long that they had neglected to safeguard the literal meaning of the textual material and had failed to mark how far they had diverged from it." Worse yet, after the time *ta'wil* came into use, "the fear of Allah was decreased, dissension increased, love disappeared and the community was divided into sects."

If this is any lesson for us, the "old hermeneutic" may not have a corner on sectarian division after all! Seeing Scripture primarily as metaphor may yet cause even more widespread division, particularly if it is used without careful discretion.

As Professor Sweetman points out, "If no discretion is used as to the texts which shall be interpreted and the persons for whom interpretation is right, confusion is introduced into the *Shari'a* [Scripture], and sects are formed, the adherents of which proclaim all others to be unbelievers." (Sound familiar?)

Looking at others in order to see ourselves involves having the courage to learn lessons from mistakes made by others before we repeat them ourselves. Will "narrative hermeneutics" deliver the spirituality and church unity it promises, or will it lead us back to the very dissension and strife we are trying to avoid?

Narrative or Myth?

Before we leave narrative behind, we simply have to talk about the late Joseph Campbell, a man who may have known more about "story" than anyone. Campbell was author of the best-selling *The Hero with a Thousand Faces* (1949) and *The Masks of God* (1959-68). Ironically, his popularity revived just shortly before he died, when he did a series of PBS interviews with Bill Moyers, called "The Power of Myth."

Those who put forward "narrative hermeneutics" are naturally wary of any connection between narrative and myth, or even *mystery* and myth, but there are simply too many parallels to completely ignore. Some of those parallels can be seen in a review of Campbell's philosophy by Belden C. Lane in *The Christian Century*.

"The first question that Campbell's work poses," says Lane, "is how to see ourselves as a people for whom myth is life and breath. How can theologians, in particular, be called back to the vitality of narrated experience? Mythology, as Campbell knew, always aims to include the listener in the tale. The story of the hero, for example, ultimately turns us back to our own experience."[6]

Is that not the same "re-creation of the biblical story in the context of our own experiences" that is at the heart of narrative theology? And note how closely Campbell's philosophy parallels current criticism of the "old hermeneutic." Says Lane,

> This is Campbell's most powerful critique of traditional Western theologies: turning all metaphors into facts, all poetry into prose, they tend toward divisiveness—supporting and validating a given social order as divinely ordained. Flexibility is abandoned for the sake of certainty. The power of myth gives way to the multiplication of propositions. Simply put, theology gets caught up too often in explaining the meaning of life instead of seeking an experience of being alive.[7]

It doesn't strain the mind to imagine what Joseph Campbell might have said about "command, example, and necessary inference!"

In his interview with Campbell, even Bill Moyers got into the swing of "pattern-bashing," saying, "These heroes of religion [Mohammed, Jesus, and Buddha] came back with the wonder of God, not with a blueprint of God."[8]

And then came the inevitable contrast between "stories" and "codes." "Religion," says Moyers, "begins with the sense of wonder and awe and the attempt to tell stories that connect us to God. Then it becomes a set of theological works in which everything is reduced to a code, to a creed."[9]

Campbell agreed. "Religion turns poetry into prose. God is *literally* up there, and this is *literally* what he thinks, and this is the way you've got to behave to get into proper relationship with that god up there."[10]

Aye, here's the rub. Now we see where narrative, story, myth, and mystery tend to lead. "Metaphor" and "poetry" permit the personalized story—each in his own heart, each in his own way. "Proposition" and "prose" tell it like it is. And none of us wants the literal truth. Give us "stories" instead.

This is where the current challenge to the Bible as a "collection of facts" once again becomes important. Listen to Campbell regarding miracles, for example:

> These stories of miracles let us know simply that this remarkable man preached of a spiritual order that is not to be identified with the merely physical order, so he could perform spiritual magic. It doesn't follow that he actually did any of these things, although of course it is possible....But the miracles of legend need not necessarily have been facts. The Buddha walked on water, as did Jesus. The Buddha ascended to heaven and returned.[11]

Is it *true* or *not true* that Jesus performed miracles as the gospel writers claim? What are the real facts? What is the real *story*? And did Buddha *really* walk on water and ascend into heaven as did Jesus? If so, then Buddha's story is just as true as Jesus' story; or, put the other way around, Jesus' story is no more compelling than Buddha's.

Where does this leave "the old, old story?" What kind of hermeneutic do we have if Jesus' death, burial, and resurrection never actually happened—if it is *just* a story, *just* myth?

Campbell's own story is that "All religions have been true *for their time*."[12] Surely, by now, that must have a familiar ring. Just how far away is that from cultural relativism, which makes every distinction possible between what the Scripture *meant* (then) and *means* (now)? Is our approach to the "women's issue," for example, so different from Campbell's perspective of story? Do we find ourselves saying that the "patriarchical" story was true *for their time*, but not for *ours*?

Unfortunately, Campbell's idea of story also fits neatly in other ways with the spirit of our age. Besides honoring Buddha along with Jesus, how much closer could Campbell get to New Age thinking than when he says, "That old man up there has been blown away. You've got to find the Force inside you. This is why Oriental gurus are so convincing to young people today. They say, 'It is in you. Go and find it.'"[13]

It's not a matter of winning a forensic debate about hermeneutics through the use of guilt by association. I don't for one minute believe that the advocates of "narrative hermeneutics" are New Agers. The point is that the idea of narrative easily lends itself to abuse, particularly when our culture has already radically shifted to the paradigm of New Age thinking which just happens (or maybe not "just happens") to elevate narrative myth over propositional truth.

Whether by its association with New Age thought, or cultural relativism, or myth and fiction, "narrative hermeneutics" plows through dangerous waters. What irony it would be if those who now recoil at being called "Campbellites" for their historical association with a rationalistic restorationist named Alexander Campbell end up having future historians calling them "Campbellites" for inheriting the legacy of a subjectivist, Christ-denying storyteller named Joseph Campbell!

Tell Me the Story of Jesus

To Bill Moyers' question, "But people ask, isn't myth a lie?" Campbell responded: "No, mythology is not a lie, mythology is poetry, it is metaphorical. It has been well said that mythology is the penultimate truth—penultimate because the ultimate cannot be put into words."

That is what I find to be so amazing about God's revelation to man. Neither myth nor metaphor—even divine metaphor—can be completely revelatory. Campbell is right: the ultimate cannot be put into words. At least not words in a book. God must have known that before we ever thought about it. What else is John chapter one all about?

"In the beginning was the Word, and the Word was with God, and the Word was God."[14] "Word" as metaphor? "Word" as narrative? Certainly, that would be a powerful image. But, for God, metaphor and narrative were not enough. So "the Word became flesh and made his dwelling among us. We have seen his glory, the glory of the One and Only, who came from the Father, full of grace and truth."[15]

When metaphor became flesh and blood, God himself came near! When what could have been merely fiction became fact, the whole world trembled!

Belden Lane has it right: "Christian theology—because of the incarnation—will always want to root an experience of the sacred in the particular and down-to-earth, being wary of vague, undifferentiated encounters with the profound."[16]

If all we have is a story, then we're no different from anybody else. *Everybody's got a story.* Ours is not simply a story, but a divine transaction between us and God. It's a story which convicts the unbeliever and brings rational man to his knees. It's a story which tells of salvation from sin secured by Jesus' death on the cross. And in that great mystery, more sublime than any myth, is the greatest love story ever told.

So let's be cautious about "narrative hermeneutics." But count me in when it comes to story. "Tell me the story of Jesus. Write on my *heart* every word!"

Part Three

TOWARD A BETTER UNDERSTANDING OF GOD'S WORD

A Not-So-New Hermeneutic For a Culture-Conscious Church

The whole series of the divine Scriptures is interpreted in a fourfold way. In all holy books one should ascertain what everlasting truths are therein intimated, what deeds are narrated, what future events are foretold, and what commands or counsels are there contained.
–The Venerable Bede

ELEVEN

Purpose, Principle, and Precedent

Let your religion be less of a theory and more of a love affair.
—G. K. Chesterton

For all the reasons discussed in Part Two, the call for an entirely new hermeneutic warrants extreme caution. Is the call motivated by our absorption into a church caught up in culture? If so, we're looking from the wrong angle. On the other hand, as Part One suggested, we may also do well to take a closer look at the "old hermeneutic" for other legitimate reasons. Perhaps there are refinements that can be made to steer us clear of previous pitfalls and help us meet the challenge of a world that has radically changed the way it thinks.

In that spirit, I propose a new formulation of the old. Call it a not-so-new hermeneutic, if you will. Instead of "command, example, and necessary inference," I wonder if we might not do well to consider "purpose, principle, and precedent" as a guide for understanding the Bible.

Before launching into a more detailed explanation of each of the three general categories, the obvious caution must be stated—that no hermeneutical formulation can ever fully "meet the test." The foremost characteristic of any articulated hermeneutic is that it is essentially human in origin—and thus doomed to inadequacy. But if we must have a hermeneutic, then we should strive to make it the best that it can possibly be. It should be as close as possible to the hermeneutics used by the prophets, the apostles, and Jesus himself.

It should also be the goal of any hermeneutic to be flexible enough to "cover all the bases"—that is, to help us interpret and apply, not only Acts and the Epistles, but also the Gospels (and indeed the Old Testament as well). It should help us focus on both the core message of redemption and sanctification in Christ, and the practical work and worship of the church.

Asking almost the impossible, it should accommodate narrative and proposition, prose and poetry, history and prophecy, parable and law—each of which, being a unique form of communication, deserves its own unique hermeneutic. What we are looking for is an umbrella hermeneutic under which each "special hermeneutic" can comfortably fit.

In striking a balance between reason and revelation, a worthy hermeneutic should call us to seek objective, "God-breathed" Truth (understandable to all who will apply themselves to the discipline of prayerful study) without minimizing the sublime mystery of the gospel. And it must be neither culture-bound nor culture-driven. A tall order indeed!

Whether *purpose, principle, and precedent* can achieve any of these goals will be for others to judge. But it is offered with all the above considerations in mind, while respectful of the "old hermeneutic" and its venerable commitment to the authority of Scripture.

Hopefully, the advantages of modifying the "old hermeneutic" will become obvious as we progress. But the intent remains the same—to get "back to the Bible." To "speak where the Bible speaks, and to be silent where the Bible is silent." To be "people of the Book," and—more importantly— people of the God of the Book!

The Importance of Purpose

As suggested in Chapter Four, our topical, proof-text, verse-by-verse tradition warrants care in our use of the "old hermeneutic." If "command, example, and necessary inference" captures the spirit of "book, chapter, and verse," what is the impact when a *verse* is unceremoniously wrenched from its proper context in a *chapter* or a *book*?

Under such circumstances, is it possible that we might have been misled regarding a given "command" or "example"? Have we, for instance, taken as a "command" some imperative that in context was never meant to be extended beyond the immediate situation? Have we too quickly seized on certain "examples," not realizing that in their own setting they were never meant to be part of the biblical pattern?

The "old hermeneutic" may have been as much a *victim* of our tradition as the perpetrator it is now claimed to be. What is the real source of the problem? Did our hermeneutic cause us to focus on individual verses, or did our anti-denominational mindset (with its topical approach to disputed issues) weaken the application of our hermeneutic? Get the context wrong, and you're bound to miss the point, no matter what hermeneutic you are using.

Proper application always follows proper exegesis. If that is a new word for you, it simply has to do with *original meaning*. Exegesis is the Who, What, When, Where, and Why of biblical texts. It's what biblical scholars do day in and day out, digging back through time like textual archaeologists to uncover the original meaning. (They obviously enjoy their work. A bumper sticker seen in the parking lot at Yale Divinity School reads, "Honk if you love exegesis!")

If exegesis could be captured in a word, the word would be *purpose*. Seen in its full and proper context, what is the *original purpose* of the passage under consideration?

The questions of Who, What, When, Where, and Why are vital. Who was writing and who was reading those early histories, laws, songs, and letters? For what purpose did the Holy Spirit allow a given passage to be a part of Scripture? What would the first readers have understood its purpose to have been? Did its purpose have limited meaning only within a certain time frame?

To do proper exegesis, we must look at historical context (What's the occasion?) and literary context (What's the point?). For those who aren't Bible scholars, the tools of exegesis are Bible handbooks, dictionaries, atlases, and commentaries. Exegesis, like archeology, requires hard work. And *careful* work. If you are intent on uncovering buried treasure, you don't bring in a two-ton shovel. Every angle has to be thoughtfully and carefully explored with godly patience.

Whereas "command, example, and necessary inference" relate most directly to what the Scriptures *mean* (for us today), "purpose" tells us more about what the Scriptures *meant* (to its original recipients). Without including any specific reference to "purpose," the "old hermeneutic" was permitted to race toward application without first being forced to determine original meaning and intent.

If the search for "purpose" had been a more visible factor to be reckoned with, the "old hermeneutic" might have been spared some of the criticism laid at its feet. Had "purpose" been more than an unstated assumption beneath the articulated formula of "command, example, and necessary inference," any temptation to abuse context might well have been avoided.

Examples of How We Might Overlook "Purpose"

Without taking into account the particular purpose of a given passage, we can easily miss the whole point of what is being said. Some examples are more graphic than others. Suppose, for instance, that we were to read the following phrase from Paul's first letter to the Corinthians: "For Christ did not send me to baptize, but to preach the gospel...."[1] Is Paul suggesting here that he is not interested in baptism, or that baptism is unimportant, or that he never personally baptized anyone?

Without looking more closely at Paul's purpose in making that statement, we might reach any of those wrong conclusions. In context, Paul is dealing with the matter of division within the church at Corinth, in which one's personal allegiance was tied to his spiritual mentor—in some instances, apparently, the particular person who happened to baptize him. Paul is simply pointing out that the teacher or baptizer is not important—only the gospel itself.

Of course, a full reading of the passage also shows that Paul did indeed personally baptize several of the Christians in Corinth, including Crispus and Gaius,[2] and the household of Stephanas.[3] Miss that detail, and we might come up with any number of wrong conclusions from Paul's more sweeping statement.

Two other passages, if read apart from their intended purposes, might make Paul out to be a real hypocrite! In Galatians, Paul says boldly: "Mark my words! I, Paul, tell you that if you let yourselves be circumcised, Christ will be of no value to you at all."[4] And yet, in Luke's account of the apostles we read that "Paul wanted to take [Timothy] along on the journey, so he circumcised him because of the Jews who lived in that area, for they all knew that his father was a Greek."[5]

If we miss the "purpose" behind what Paul said to the Galatians, we have to conclude that Christ was no longer of any value to Timothy once he had been circumcised. Ironically, the apparent conflict between these two passages turns out to be an exegetical *help*. By holding one passage up to the other, we can better understand Paul's point to the Galatians that circumcision—itself a religiously neutral act—can void the gospel of Christ if it is intended to symbolize a return to the Mosaic law. Truly, "the Bible is its own best interpreter."

One final example ought to be obvious from its mere statement, but a failure to note the intended purpose could work mischief. It's Paul's controversial statement, "I do not permit a woman to teach or to have authority over a man; she must be silent."[6] Taken alone, the passage might suggest that there are no circumstances under which a woman may teach. But is that really what Paul had in mind?

It takes only a quick glance at Paul's letter to Titus to see that he encourages older women to "teach what is good" so that they can "train the younger women."[7] Again, the two passages taken together help to make sense of the "purpose" behind Paul's prohibition—not that women are to remain silent in all instances, but that they are not to take an authoritative lead in teaching men.

Miss the "purpose," and we miss the original intent. Miss the original intent, and we risk missing the correct application of Scripture to our own circumstances. Proper exegesis is basically a matter of care and discernment in the way that we read Scripture.

Surely, this is what Paul meant when he told Timothy (and also ourselves?) to be one who "correctly handles the word of truth."[8] I like the more well-known rendering: "rightly dividing." That's what we must do, if we are to truly understand God's Word. It's absolutely critical that we *divide* the Scriptures according to the purpose for which they were intended—some being meant only for those to whom the statement was originally made; others being a message for all who would believe.

Naturally, we will not all "divide" the Scriptures in the same way, even those of us who share many of the same biblical perspectives. But it is crucial that we keep asking all those exegetical questions of Who, What, When, Where, and Why? *Who, What, When, Where, and Why?* Stop asking those questions, and we may miss the whole "purpose" of the exercise.

A Point Well Taken

Some of those who reviewed the first drafts of this book have pointed out that I haven't been sufficiently helpful in filling in all the blanks regarding the process of exegesis. Of course they are right. But that is also another book (or books) which others more qualified than myself have already written. Nor do I wish to fall into the trap of presuming greater precision than can fairly be offered, lest I be accused of fostering yet another formulistic scientific method for determining biblical authority.

In calling our attention to "purpose," I simply wish to draw us back to the basics of careful scholarship. In that call, I join hands with those who are urging us—for all the right reasons—to rethink how we study Scripture. It is under the category of "purpose" that most of their concerns can be satisfied. If we can get closer to the *original* purpose of the inspired writer, we are that much closer to understanding the passage's *present* meaning for our own situation.

If this seems like a cop-out, or appears to beg the question, nevertheless I hope at the very least to have dignified the importance of a process which all too easily can be ignored. (For those who seek more practical application, Chapter 12 is designed to further explore how we determine "purpose.")

From "Commands" to "Principles"

Once we have correctly determined the original purpose of a given passage in the biblical text, the next step is to evaluate how it is to be implemented in our own situation. Under the "old hermeneutic," we've leaned heavily on whatever "commands" are given in Scripture. (There is probably no need here to distinguish between "old law" and "new." For reasons outside the scope of this book, there is general agreement that not every "command" under the Law of Moses is to be obeyed in Christ.)

Our respect for scriptural commands comes from any number of passages which actually use the word *command* as an indication of intended authority. We might think, for instance, of Paul's letter to Timothy:

> Although I hope to come to you soon, I am writing you these instructions so that, if I am delayed, you will know how people ought to conduct themselves in God's household, which is the church of the living God, the pillar and foundation of the truth....*Command and teach these things.*[9]

If there were ever any doubt as to the true source of biblical commands, Paul goes out of his way on occasion to attribute his directives to divine origin. He says, for instance, "To the married I give this command (not I, but the Lord)...."[10]

As if to ensure the force of divine command when it is meant to be authoritative, Paul is careful to point out when his instructions are *not* the Lord's commands: "I say this as a concession, not as a command."[11] And "To the rest I say this (I, not the Lord)...."[12] Or, most interesting of all, "*In my judgment*, she is happier if she stays as she is—*and I think that I too have the Spirit of God.*"[13]

Lest we think of "commands" as legalistic and negative, we hear John telling us, "This is love for God: to obey his commands. And his commands are not burdensome, for everyone born of God overcomes the world. This is the victory that has overcome the world, even our faith."[14] When was the last time we thought of "commands" having anything to do with *love* and *faith?*

Not Every Imperative Is a Command Performance

That said, it's no secret that we do not treat all biblical "commands" the same. Consider just two examples. First, there is Paul's instruction: "Greet one another with a holy kiss."[15] Because the kiss is not our normal form of greeting, we settle for a holy hug or handshake.

More than that, of course, Paul's statement is not even in the same category as his other instructive "commands." His intent is not to enjoin any point of doctrine, but merely to close his various letters on a note of Christian fellowship. We know this in the same common-sense way that we recognize a personal note at the end of a business letter.

Unless the content of the note should indicate otherwise, we naturally take it as merely incidental communication. "Greet one another with a holy kiss" is of the same literary species as "Bring the cloak that I left with Carpus"[16] and "Do your best to get here before winter,"[17] both of which we find at the close of Paul's second letter to Timothy. From this instance alone (if not so easily from others), we recognize that not all imperative statements are tantamount to commands.

In yet another example, Paul's teaching about women covering their heads when praying or prophesying has the ring of a doctrinal command: "If anyone wants to be contentious about this, we have no other practice—nor do the churches of God."[18] Yet, relatively few women among our fellowship wear anything like a veil in worship. Why is that?

First of all, if ever there were a difficult passage, 1 Corinthians 11:3-16 has to be in the running. Is the "covering" to be understood as a veil; or the woman's own hair? What is the origin of the wearing of veils to which Paul refers? Would a veil today reflect the principle of male headship in the same way that it did in the first century?

In order to make any sense of this passage, one has to carefully consider the historical setting (*purpose*, once again).

Women were already wearing veils as a matter of custom, without any hint of divine mandate. Despite the earlier-cited language which leaves no doubt about the veil's importance as a first-century practice, what we sometimes overlook is the fact that nowhere, either in 1 Corinthians 11 or elsewhere, is there any specific command telling women to *put on* the veil. Therefore, it is clear that, whatever else he intended to say, Paul wasn't *initiating* the wearing of veils. The context suggests that he was merely prohibiting the *removal* of veils, probably because it made a wrong statement about male headship.

The point of the illustration is that, if we're not careful in our use of "commands," we can end up mistaking just what it is that is being commanded. Given the proper context, Paul's concern regarding the veil comes out almost opposite from what appears at first blush. Put into the precise form of a command, undoubtedly the message is: "If you're taking off your veil in the mistaken belief that the principle of male headship no longer applies, don't!" First and foremost, it is the principle of male spiritual leadership that is being commanded.

From this same illustration, we see the first reason why thinking in terms of "principle" may be more helpful than thinking in terms of "command." Thinking categorically in terms of "commands" can be misleading. The problem is that we can get misled by the sheer grammatical appearance of certain statements. "If it *looks like* a command," we say to ourselves, "then it *must* be a command!"

Yet, in this instance, what *looks like* an open-ended "command" has its intended application defined by a larger "principle." (The veil is being commanded only because its *removal* violates the principle of male spiritual leadership.) If we're not careful, we get fooled by the *grammatical form* and automatically assume a particular application of the "command" which was never intended. For that reason, looking for "principles" instead of looking simply for "commands" can minimize the confusion arising out of some of the more difficult passages.

Seeing 1 Corinthians 11 more in terms of "principle" than "command" does not change the authoritative nature of that which is being taught. There is no reason to conclude that it contains a directive which we are now free to ignore. Wherever women in the church wear special head coverings as symbols of submission to male spiritual leadership (as is the case even today in many congregations), then Paul's directive still applies. It would be just as wrong for them to quit wearing the covering in outspoken rejection of male headship as for the women in Corinth to have done so.

Rather than leading to more ambiguity than "commands," as one might suspect, biblical "principles" are never susceptible to the temptation to overwork an imperative statement merely because of its grammatical form. And far from being any less authoritative, "principles" take us ever closer to the heart of what "commands" are all about.

"Principles" Where There Are No "Commands"

The "head coverings" passage illustrates yet another advantage of "principles" over "commands." In addition to the more overarching principle of male headship, we can see that there is a lower-level principle at work as well. Without any explicit "command" in this particular regard, it is clear from Paul's instructions that Christian women should do nothing which could be interpreted, in terms of their own culture, as a protest to the larger principle.

This "lesser principle" causes us to ask, for example, "What is it in our own twentieth-century society that would make a wrong statement about male headship? If not the taking off of a veil or other covering, what might be its modern-day equivalent?" If we concentrate solely on specific "commands," we might never ask ourselves such questions and miss out on important *unstated* biblical principles. The fact is that we may be under obligation to a spiritual "principle" even when we might not be able to point specifically to any articulated "command."

We see this even more clearly in the kind of teaching that Jesus did, which was not always couched in imperative language. For example, consider Jesus' words, "If anyone gives even a cup of cold water to one of these little ones because he is my disciple, I tell you the truth, he will certainly not lose his reward."[19] Strictly speaking, there is no "command" here. And yet the principle ought to be clear, whether it's a cup of cold water given to a first-century Judean, or a bowl of hot soup given to a twentieth-century Eskimo!

It's not fossilization of some wooden "commandment" that Jesus intended, but whatever moral equivalent might be applicable under the obvious "principle" involved.

Caution, Caution—Always Caution!

Naturally, what we gain from this new perspective we will lose ten times over if we assume that principles never have more specific commands attached. The idea is not to ignore specific biblical commands, but to reach further and make sure that we connect them properly to any overarching principles. Each is a contextual safeguard to the other.

The dragon waiting in the alley to devour us at this point is the notion that we are free to ignore specific commands as long as we honor the principle. Take, for example, Paul's instruction in 1 Timothy 2 that a woman not teach or have authority over a man. Are we free to say that a woman can do public teaching as long as she honors the principle of male spiritual leadership? (More and more Christians are taking this position, saying that a woman may do public teaching and preaching as long as she is "released" to do so, either by the elders or by her husband.)

And can we say of the Lord's Supper that it's not the bread and fruit of the vine that's important, but only the principle of spiritual "sustenance"? Or of baptism that it's not the literal act of being immersed that is being commanded in Acts 2:38, but the principle of obedience?

Even taken on its face, such an attitude makes no sense. What honor do we give to the principle if we ignore the specific commands which are given for the purpose of implementing it? Regardless of whatever overarching principle may be involved, specific commands simply cannot be ignored with impunity.

"Principles" Can Provide a Greater Motivation

In order to illustrate the next advantage of thinking in terms of "principles," let's turn to another primary passage. In many congregations, it doesn't seem right if someone doesn't say prior to the collection, "We've been commanded to give of our means on the first day of the week as we have prospered."

However, a closer look at 1 Corinthians 16 may surprise us—especially if we are careful once again to look for original "purpose." Taken together with Paul's second letter to the Corinthians, an altogether different picture emerges than the rather austere "command" for either the Corinthians or us to include in weekly worship "laying by in store on the first day of the week."

From Paul's second letter (chapter 8), it is clear that the collection was not a command from Paul, but a generous response to a particular need:

> I am not commanding you, but I want to test the sincerity of your love by comparing it with the earnestness of others....And here is my advice about what is best for you in this matter: Last year you were the first not only to give but also to have the desire to do so. Now finish the work, so that your eager willingness to do it may be matched by your completion of it, according to your means.[20]

Automatically seeing "commands" in any imperative language we might encounter in Scripture tends to close our eyes to the complete picture. (One can only wonder how Paul might react to our transformation of his words of encouragement into a formal plank of our doctrinal platform.)

Rather than legislating a universal command for all Christians, Paul's instructions were simply a practical means of implementing a special collection which the Corinthians themselves had volunteered on behalf of the poor saints in Jerusalem. (If we insist on a "command-oriented" view of the passage, consistency would require that any money we today "lay by in store" must also await Paul's arrival and be taken to Jerusalem.)

There is no reason to fear that church collections are somehow, therefore, unbiblical. If we no longer have what might legitimately be called a "command," we are still left with an "example" of considerable weight—or, more importantly, with a number of spiritual principles which may even enhance all the more our understanding of Christian giving.

To begin with, having the *desire* to give may itself be the most significant principle to be derived, in sharp contrast to our giving only because we are obeying a "command." By observing the *principle* rather than the *command*, we are likely to come to a fuller appreciation of the weekly contribution "...as a generous gift, not as one grudgingly given."

And, of course, there is also the principle of giving according to our individual prosperity, so that no one might be unduly burdened.[21] And there is also the principle of accountability in the use of the funds, together with the important principle of preserving proper appearances in handling church finances.[22] (How many congregations have followed the *"command"* to give, but ignored the *principle* of good stewardship?)

Let's face it, it's not always easy to be a "cheerful giver" when the stated object is to comply with a *command* to give. Such a focus robs us of our better instincts. By contrast, principles have a way of motivating us far beyond what we tend to perceive as more-burdensome commands.

The dynamic we're talking about here is played out in wholesome homes between parent and child. The parent-child relationship points to some of the problems we face when we over-emphasize such words as "authoritative," "binding," and "limiting." During childhood, certainly, our father is over us and we must respect his authority. Yet, properly speaking, the emphasis in the relationship is love. In a proper parent-child relationship, we think of comfort, security, and a desire to please, not simply of rules and regulations.

So it should be with our Father in heaven. And so it *can* be when we move from giving exclusive attention to "commands" and see the greater motivation which comes from godly "principles."

"Principles" Can Reflect Examples As Well As Commands

Yet another advantage of biblical principles is that they have sufficient scope to include both "commands" and "examples." It is easy, of course, to see how specific commands can form the basis for an unstated principle, or indeed reflect a principle that is clearly articulated in Scripture. But the same can also be true of biblical examples. In fact, the more examples we have of a given practice—particularly if they cross the lines of both Jewish and Christian dispensations—the more likely we are to have discovered a transcendent spiritual principle.

Interestingly enough, a principle may be derived from biblical examples even when those examples, in and of themselves, might not rise to the level of so-called "binding examples." For instance, if Old Testament examples are not to be regarded as "binding" (authoritative), they nevertheless tell us much about spiritual principles.

As 1 Corinthians 16 and its related passages remind us, what looks like a "command" may actually, from our perspective, turn out to be an important "example." What's helpful about thinking in terms of a "principle" is that there is less pressure on us to decide whether it is a "command" or whether it is an "example." All we really need to know in most instances is that we are being called to obey one or more spiritual principles that God has instituted.

If we are forced to distinguish between "commands" and "examples," the task can sometimes seem impossible. As a kind of practical exercise, you may find it interesting to read this mixed selection from Paul's first letter to Timothy and try to decide which parts are more suited to "command" and which to "example." (If you're thinking ahead, you might also wish to be alert to any appropriate "principles" which are suggested.)

> Until I come, devote yourself to the public reading of Scripture, to preaching and to teaching....Watch your life and doctrine closely. Persevere in them, because if you do, you will save both yourself and your hearers....Do not rebuke an older man harshly, but exhort him as if he were your father. Treat younger men as brothers, older women as mothers, and younger women as sisters, with absolute purity.

> Stop drinking only water, and use a little wine because of your stomach and your frequent illnesses.

> In the presence of God and of Christ Jesus, who will judge the living and the dead, and in view of his appearing and his kingdom, I give you this charge: Preach the Word; be prepared in season and out of season; correct, rebuke and encourage—with great patience and careful instruction....But you, keep your head in all situations, endure hardship, do the work of an evangelist, discharge all the duties of your ministry.[23]

Okay, be honest! Into which category did you put Paul's imperative words instructing Timothy to use a little wine? Is it a command for us to follow? Is it even an example? Because of the highly personal nature of these instructions, we tend to give them less play than Paul's instructions in the same letter regarding, say, the qualifications for elders.

But, surely, there is something of significance that even we are meant to carry away from this apostolic correspondence. Among other compelling principles, there is much to learn, for instance, about closely watching our life and doctrine, and about the manner in which we are to rebuke those who are older. And what a challenging set of principles was laid down for those who would proclaim the gospel!

Limiting ourselves to commands and examples has the effect of reducing the canon of Scripture to only two forms of teaching, when the canon also contains a veritable goldmine of spiritual principles meant for our edification. Whether technically a "command" or technically an "example" (or neither), overarching spiritual principles have the advantage of broadening our vision of what it means to follow apostolic teaching.

"Principles" Cover All the Bases

In a similar vein, Paul told the Corinthians that he had received the thoughts of God through the Holy Spirit, "not in words taught us by human wisdom but in words taught by the Spirit, expressing spiritual truths in spiritual words."[24] *Spiritual truths!* Not "commands" in every instance. Not always "examples." But spiritual truths—*spiritual principles*—that can be seen throughout the entire Bible, be it in story and metaphor or in law and letter. Moving from "commands" to "principles" immediately gives us flexibility in understanding the various parts of Scripture, whether prose or poetry, prophecy or proverb, Gospels or Revelation.

Thinking in terms of "principle" is not at all something new for us. It's really what we've done all along without giving it a hermeneutical label. Consider, for example, the sin of lying and falsehood. Have we ever considered it a sin solely because some "command" in one of the epistles prohibits it? ("Do not lie to each other, since you have taken off your old self with its practices," Colossians 3:9.) Or because we have an "example" in Acts where lying brought severe punishment for Ananias and Sapphira? ("You have not lied to men but to God," Acts 5:1-4.)

To the contrary, we have always recognized falsehood to be violative of the spiritual principle of truthfulness whether we saw it in *law* ("Do not lie," Leviticus 19:11); in the *psalms* ("Their throat is an open grave; with their tongue they speak deceit," Psalm 5:9); in the *proverbs* ("A truthful witness gives honest testimony, but a false witness tells lies," Proverbs 12:17); in *prophecy* ("Truth has perished; it has vanished from their lips," Jeremiah 7:28); or in the *Gospels* ("You belong to your father, the devil....When he lies, he speaks his native language, for he is a liar and the father of lies," John 8:44,45).

Old Testament or New—psalm, proverb, or prophecy—the truths of God permeate the entire fabric of Scripture. Relative to the whole of revelation, only rarely are they couched in anything so specific as a "command." It is in the idea of "principle," then, that we find a hermeneutic which encompasses the complexity, diversity, and trustworthiness of divine pattern.

From "Example" to "Precedent"

Under the "old hermeneutic," the second major way in which we have found biblical authority is through divine "example." And justifiably so. The pattern principle simply has no substitute. The only alternative to *following* pattern is *ignoring* pattern, and we do that only at the risk of rejecting apostolic guidance which itself came from the Holy Spirit. If we don't accept that premise, of course, then nothing about "pattern" or "example" makes any sense whatsoever.

But, just as with "commands," we must be very careful to discern whether we are encountering an authoritative "example," or whether we are merely encountering some incidental biblical "occurrence." Not every occurrence is to be considered an "example." There are examples, and then there are *examples*!

To cite only a few *non-examples*, there is, first of all, the upper room in which the Lord's Supper was instituted. Are we to meet in an upper room when we partake of the Supper?[25] There's also the instance where Paul cut his hair in connection with making a vow.[26] Are we to cut our hair in the same way—or indeed to make similar vows? And, of course, there is the example of Paul blinding Elymas the sorcerer.[27] Are we supposed to inflict injury on those who oppose the gospel?

Sorting out examples from non-examples is, once again, mostly a matter of determining textual *purpose.* We're back to Who, What, When, Where, and Why? The original circumstances in which an occurrence took place generally dictate how authoritative that occurrence is meant to be for us today. Unfortunately, the very nature of examples (as compared with specific propositional statements) makes it difficult to be sure in every case.

That is why it may be worthwhile considering a difference in focus, from mere "examples" to the more value-laden term *precedent.* The question is not, "Do we have an example?" but "Do we have an example that should be considered *authoritative?*" That's really what we've meant all along when we've referred to "*binding* examples."

Interestingly, *precedent* is the word most often used by the first restorers in our movement. The goal of restoration was not to reinstitute the riding of donkeys or the wearing of robes and sandals. It was to reach back far enough to avoid human innovation in Christian worship, and even farther back to capture the work and worship of New Testament

Christians as they were guided by the Holy Spirit through the apostles' doctrine.

Before we discuss further how we can determine when an example is authoritative, and thus precedent, we need to quickly look at two types of "examples" which fall into lesser categories. The first type includes biblical examples that are "permissive" without being required. Included in this category, for example, would be the communal sharing in which the fledgling church participated immediately following Pentecost.[28]   Although not required of Christians today (unless perhaps a similar need should arise), a Christian community in which all property is held in common would not violate any spiritual principles.

Other "permissive" examples would include "meeting from house to house";[29] having a fellowship meal along with the Lord's Supper;[30] supporting widows;[31] and having "paid" elders.[32]

The second category includes incidental occurrences and illustrations which do not even have the look of authoritativeness. Do we hear many people urging, for example, that sermons should last until midnight?[33]   Or that we should literally tear our clothes as the apostles did when faced with blasphemous conduct?[34] Or that proper observance of the Lord's Supper includes meeting in an upper room?[35]

But, then, maybe I'm overly optimistic in thinking incidentals are always so obvious. How can one possibly explain the reasoning of those who insist that there be *but one cup* for the communion! I can think of no rule of hermeneutics that can be a complete safeguard against abandonment of the kind of reasoning we use when we read the Sunday paper.

These occurrences clearly have the look of circumstantial coincidence. And in most instances, thankfully, our own good sense will know which is which. The more difficult cases are those in which examples pertain directly to the work and worship of the church. For even among these, the question remains: Which examples are *precedent*, and which are not?

Relating "Examples" to Principles

In precedent, as opposed to mere example, we are looking for *justifiable reliance*. Is there something about a given example on which we can rely for our own spiritual guidance? To start with, an example cannot be seen as normative, or as precedent, unless we can first draw some obvious rule from the example. Put another way, we must first conclude that the example "stands for" something—some rule or principle. If it does, then in most cases we can rely on it in the same way we would rely on any other rule or principle.

Of course, the best way to determine whether an example contains within it a kind of "rule" is to see whether there is already some spiritual law or principle that has been articulated in Scripture independently of the example. For instance, the Lord's Supper is not only participated in as a matter of sheer occurrence, but there is specific teaching about its theological significance as well as certain practical instructions as to how it is to be observed.

Another rule of thumb is that examples having obvious *universal application*, rather than limited or special circumstances, are more likely to be precedent. Compare, for instance, the widespread practice of baptism with the special circumstances surrounding Paul's vow and headshaving. Which is more likely to be just an occurrence-type "example" and which more likely to be compelling "precedent"?

Universal application can also be seen in examples which represent *stability of teaching over time*. That's why practices which carry over from Jewish to Christian worship (like prayer and songs of praise) are particularly suitable as precedent. On the other hand, in Chapter 13 we will consider the implications to be drawn when a given example of Jewish worship comes to an abrupt halt in Christian worship. The *absence of example* may be as precedent-setting as any actual example itself.

"Necessary Inference" Comes Along For the Ride

That last point about the *absence of example* brings us, finally, to the third component of the "old hermeneutic," generally known as "necessary inference." The beauty of focusing on principles and precedents rather than commands and examples is that we no longer need be haunted by the controversies which too often have surrounded "necessary inference."

When all we have are rather wooden "commands" and narrowly-selected "examples," we are constantly having to fill in gaps in those areas of Christian work and worship where we have neither "specific commands" nor "binding examples" to direct us. (May we use song books? Is it proper to have a kitchen in the church building? Must an elder resign if his wife dies?) That's where we've often run into trouble trying to decide which inferences are "necessary" and which are not. The good news is that, with the combination of "principle" and "precedent," even fairly yawning gaps in practical application tend to be filled in.

Think of it like a bridge across a broad expanse. Where specific commands and authoritative examples provide crucial structural support vertically, the inherently wider scope of principle and precedent can horizontally span the entire breadth of Christian worship and living.

When we think in terms of principle and precedent, we have already taken into account any so-called "necessary inferences"—and done so (most importantly) in a manner consistent with original purpose. Whether certain biblical statements are couched in imperative language (*looking* like a "command") or whether they are simply biblical truths coming from, say, the psalms or proverbs, we have already *inferred* certain principles that obviously were meant to apply to us today. (We saw that demonstrated in the exercise regarding the principle of truthfulness.) Likewise, in moving from "mere examples" to "precedent," we have already *inferred* that those particular examples are authoritative.

The conversion of Cornelius[36] gives us a wonderful illustration of how we proceed from inferences. In one respect, of course, it was really the conversion of *Peter,* who, despite "the great commission,"[37] did not at first understand the principle of universal grace. When he finally got hold of the principle, Peter needed no further specific commandment. ("I now realize how true it is that God does not show favoritism but accepts men from every nation who fear him and do what is right."[38]) Once he got hold of the principle, the inferences were already built-in: God accepted Cornelius (a specific example turned precedent), and God accepts any Gentile who believes and obeys (a principle for all time).

Interestingly, Peter shows us precisely how he had inferred the principle.   In defense of his participation in Cornelius' conversion, Peter later responds to his Jewish critics, saying, "So if God gave them the same gift as he gave us, who believed in the Lord Jesus Christ, who was I to think that I could oppose God?"[39] From the *gift*, Peter had inferred the *grace*.

And isn't that how we all think in any event? Every day we make hundreds of inferences from what people say and do.   We *live* by inferences! As a matter of fact, without inferences, the Bible itself has no meaning to us at all. Consider for a moment that not one command in the Bible is aimed directly at any of us. No command or example has our name specifically written on it. Nevertheless we rightly infer that what God directed others to do is equally our duty unless the sense of context indicates otherwise.

For example, although none of us living today were commanded to "go and make disciples of all nations,"[40] we rightly infer the imperative of evangelism. And although we ourselves have not been directly commanded to "repent and be baptized," as were the men and women who first heard those words on Pentecost,[41] we rightly infer the importance of baptism in our own conversion.

Given the nature of inference generally, we have no pressing need to further include "necessary inference" in any formulation of our hermeneutic. In "purpose, principle, and precedent," all *necessary* inferences are automatically built-in. Built-in, that is, if we've done our homework. Built-in if we've got our principles and precedents right.   Get those wrong, of course, and we are likely to make costly mistakes in our attempts to apply principle and precedent to our current situation.

Building On a Commitment to Scripture

The "old hermeneutic" has always been the right idea, and certainly captures the right attitude toward the authority of Scripture.   By God's grace, a not-so-new hermeneutic of *purpose, principle, and precedent* can serve to bring out the best in our hermeneutical heritage and lead us confidently toward whatever future we face.

TWELVE

Applying the Not-So-New Hermeneutic

The way to understand the Scriptures and all theology is to become holy. It is to be under the authority of the Spirit.
—Martyn Lloyd-Jones

On a recent Sunday evening, I left my little English cottage to travel to a village some ten miles cross-country. Normally, I take the backroads through two small villages. On this night, freezing fog limited visibility to some 50 feet, and I found driving almost impossible. The winding country lanes had no markings, and, naturally, very little traffic even at the busiest of times. On this night, there were no other cars venturing forth to give me company.

Faced with the task of feeling my way along under those treacherous circumstances, I turned back to go home. But as I reached the short stretch of main highway that led from the country lane back to my village, it occurred to me that I could see the white stripes down the middle of the highway, and also the reflective "cat's eyes" that illuminated the center of the road. That gave me encouragement to continue on the main highway in a rather round-about way to my destination.

It wasn't long before I came up behind two or three other cars going in my direction. Between being able to follow their taillights, and having the center of the road well marked out, the remainder of my journey was slow, but sure. Without the road markings and assistance of other cars up ahead, I would never have made it. With their help, I was able to make my appointment and return home in complete safety.

It occurred to me that my experience in the fog explains a lot about our search for God. In the midst of the fog which surrounds our human existence, finding our way through life can be as uncertain as the first road I took without any markings. Directionless, we are on our own, left to creep along for fear of running into the ditch. But a life that has a center stripe down the middle of the highway, as it were, gives us direction, safety, and assurance. By God's grace, what seems to be an impossible destination becomes attainable.

This theological analogy suggests a similar analogy with hermeneutics. The "center stripe" of interpretation is the collective leading of the many biblical principles found in Scripture. Taken together—one by one, "mile after mile," as it were—those individual stripes form the bright line that keeps us in the right way—the way of Him who *is* the Way.

Similarly, the taillights of the cars ahead of me are analogous to the precedent of biblical examples. Naturally, I didn't blindly follow the other cars wherever they went. One by one, the other cars would turn off the main road for other destinations. And when they did, I did not follow them. I continued to follow their lead only so far as they themselves kept to the center line of the highway which I knew was the main road.

That, in a nutshell, is the idea of precedent—where we follow the lead of those men and women of faith who have gone before us. We don't follow their lead blindly. (There is no call for imitating the apostles when they were disputing about who among them was the greatest.) But we follow them as they appear to be consistent with the guiding principles which are reflected out of the pages of Holy Writ.

The Coherence Factor

The convergence of principle and precedent, as seen in the illustration of the center stripe and the taillights up ahead, introduces us to what might be called *the coherence factor*. I might have managed to follow the center stripe on my own, with no other cars around, but I tell you it was a great relief to be able to follow someone else's lead. With such a pattern, I had the double assurance of knowing I was always on the right road.

Once purpose, principle, and precedent are individually understood, the idea of *coherence* becomes important. Coherence calls for a consistency between purpose, principle, and precedent—especially the latter two. When achieved, coherence promotes reliability, predictability, and evenhandedness.

Where we have *both* principle *and* precedent, we have the strongest case for biblical authority. Consider, for instance, the passages which give double support to baptism, the Lord's Supper, prayer, and benevolence. Each of these is specifically directed through biblical principles, and each is backed by multiple examples of implementation.

On the other hand, where one of the two (usually principle) is missing, the case is weaker. Consider, here, the idea of Christians having all things in common, as did the first believers following Pentecost. Standing on its own, the passage in Acts is straightforward and unambiguous:

> All the believers were together and had everything in common. Selling their possessions and goods, they gave to anyone as he had need.[1]

There is no question but that this biblical example suggests the principle of fellowship and sharing—even to the point of sacrifice, if necessary. But whether it additionally suggests a requirement that Christians today live in some kind of a communal arrangement is highly doubtful.

Looking under the heading of "purpose" at the historical context, it is clear that the circumstances facing these first believers were unique, to say the least. Never before nor since has there been anything quite like that joyous Pentecost, with its sudden influx of the faithful from distant homelands finding themselves short-handed as they stayed on to participate in this revolutionary fellowship.

The case is further weakened by the fact that we have no clear "principle" mandating communal living for believers. In all of Scripture, there is not a hint of anything like Marxist or communist theory, as some have suggested from this passage. Note, too, the lack of any other supporting precedents. The less that can be found by way of principle, the more that is demanded by way of precedent, and *vice versa*.

Whereas clear principle without precedent, or clear precedent without principle, may alone be sufficient authority for our spiritual leading, the strongest and safest course will always be found in the coherence factor. Tie together the bundle of "purpose," "principle," and "precedent," and you can rest assured that God is trying to tell us something! Anything less, and we must proceed with more caution.

Dealing With Apparent Conflicts

One of the most difficult areas of biblical interpretation is where there appear to be collisions between two or more biblical *principles*, or between two *precedents*, or between *principle* and *precedent*. If the perceived conflict is between two or more principles, we should first consider that there are two kinds of biblical principles—*aspirational* and *directive*.

Aspirational principles are such principles as love, faith, unity, justice, and truth. They are so basic to Scripture that individual passages hardly need be cited. Typically, they provide the framework for more specific guidelines that are meant to put meat on the bare bones of our noblest aspirations and make possible the practical day-to-day implementation of those higher principles. "What does love mean?" "How does faith act?" "In what specific ways do we do justice?"

Directive principles, on the other hand, may look more like *rules*. Consider, for example, Paul's summary following a long list of specific instructions to the Corinthians about marriage and separation:

> Nevertheless, each one should retain the place in life that the Lord assigned to him and to which God has called him. This is the *rule* I lay down in all the churches.[2]

And what could be more rule-like than these instructions about the role of women in worship?

> As in all the congregations of the saints,
> women should remain silent in the churches.
> They are not allowed to speak, but must be in
> submission, as the Law says....If anybody thinks
> he is a prophet or spiritually gifted, let him
> acknowledge that what I am writing to you is the
> Lord's command.[3]

In the face of such specific instructions, it is difficult to dismiss their directiveness by simply referring to such aspirational principles as "justice-love." Can justice and love so easily negate Paul's specific instruction, "I do not permit a woman to teach or have authority over a man"? The God of "justice" and "love" would hardly tell us to do something specific that would violate a more overarching principle.

This is where we have to make sure that we are not overlooking any other truths which are equally, if not more, compelling. (Leveling all principles and rules can be just as pernicious as leveling all facts and examples.)

If one includes *obedience* along with justice and love as one of the overarching biblical truths, we know that obedience is always paramount to love, at least if our idea of love involves *disobedience.* ("To obey is better than to sacrifice...."[4]) The fact is that obedience will always be a matter of justice and love, because God never asks us to do that which is unjust or unloving.

There's a reminder here that the ambiguity of the overarching truths is always ripe for subjective definition. What *we* consider to be love or justice (and, more particularly these days, equality) is too often merely a cultural definition. Indeed, that is the safeguard of having more specifically-articulated biblical principles and their derivative rules.

Unfortunately, I realize that any failure to appreciate that last paragraph could be the Achilles heel of purpose, principle, and precedent. I can already see some folks who will love the word "principle" because they think it allows them more room to maneuver than they now have with specific, hard-and-fast "commands." All I can say is that, for those who may be bent on avoiding the authority of Scripture, no hermeneutic is going to stand in their way.

How Principles Enhance "Rules"

Biblical truths come to us in a hierarchy of guidelines. The higher "aspirational principles" illuminate the more specific "directive principles" which in turn illuminate even more specific "rules."   In this sense, principles are like explanations for the rules, the general explaining the more specific. (Those who are suspicious of inductive reasoning should be comforted in knowing that there is not always a move from the specific to the general.)

But principles are not merely explanatory in nature. Like "rules," they are directive and instructive. They teach and they inform, but they also "insist," even without the presence of any clear rules which might be drawn from them for a given situation. Having love and doing justice are not mere platitudes. They are qualities God insists that we have! ("And what does the Lord *require* of you? To act justly and to love mercy and to walk humbly with your God."[5])

What, then, is the relationship between "principles" and "rules"? Principles are compelling even though they do not always fully determine every matter to which they might be relevant.   For example, "justice-love" prohibits *abuse* of role relationships, but does not fully define what those relationships are to be. Does having love for our fellow man automatically tell us how we ought to respond to civil government? Did loving God automatically answer the Gentiles' questions about eating meat which had been sacrificed to idols?

Rules, on the other hand, rarely ever on their own fully determine *every* case to which they are relevant. For example, the specific rules laid down for women in the worship of the first-century church do not address any number of very practical questions we have today: Should women pass communion trays, read scripture, join in leading chain prayers, etc? To answer those questions, we need more than the few rules we are given. That's where the *principle* of male spiritual leadership comes in. It gives us a point of reference where there are questions which more specific biblical guidelines fail to address.

There is a flip-side to that coin, as well. The principle of male spiritual leadership *in the abstract* wouldn't have given

us sufficient guidelines to fully know the kinds of circumstances to which it should be applied. Therefore, specific
rules and examples of practical implementation are provided
in order to show us the principle's inner workings and outer
boundaries.

What principles do that rules cannot do is to bridge
centuries of cultural change and always be applicable to the
church in any culture—not that culture determines the principle, but that principle answers the continuing needs of
culture as it evolves. The beauty of Scripture is that it gives us
just the right balance between principle and precedent. Too
much specificity of principle (seen merely as arbitrary rules)
and we would be culture-bound to the first century. That was
the problem faced by Jewish Christians who wanted to hang
on to the Law of Moses. They could never be fully free of its
yoke. Yet, too little specificity of precedent (with no examples
whatever to follow) and we could be at the mercy of our own
culture—in too many ways a *God-denying* culture.

Overruling Principle

As culture changes, there is a temptation to alter external
forms of worship so as to be more culturally relevant. In order
to alter the outer forms, it often becomes necessary to
minimize the impact of the scriptures which initially established those forms. That, of course, is a nice way of saying
that, at least in some instances, we must *overrule* Scripture
in order to achieve the intended result.

When it comes to overruling either principle or precedent,
we are foolish to proceed solely on the basis that it is no longer
consistent with cultural expectations. The danger of replacing God's wisdom with the collective wisdom of a God-
denying secular society is why we have to trust in God's
leading through revelation to the fullest extent that we can—
often even in the smaller details which we might hastily
conclude are culturally irrelevant.

It's interesting how overruling occurs. Rarely is it the
bold, sweeping renunciation of a given principle or precedent. Typically, it is more Darwinian in nature—a kind of
"creeping gradualism." Typically, too, it happens less *doctrinally* than *practically*.

Initially, you see just the first tiny steps away from the established norm, then gradually a series of incremental steps which end up miles away from where we used to be. At that point, of course, someone has to step in and make an attempt at justifying the change (perhaps even by calling for a whole new hermeneutic!). But usually the rule or practice itself has been overturned long before any new practice is officially recognized. A kind of transformation may have taken place before any formal announcement of any change.

We can see this process taken to the extreme in the historical development of the papacy. All it took at first was the slightest change in the role of elders, then the loss of congregational autonomy, then hierarchy, and finally the Pope. Closer to home, we have seen the seemingly insignificant battle over the Missionary Society result in a loss of congregational autonomy and finally the denominational development of both the Christian Church and the Disciples of Christ.

Transformation does not always happen gradually or incrementally. A classic example of a more immediate metamorphosis took place in one congregation when the elders agreed to a request for a class discussing the role of women in the church, including whether women should teach mixed adult classes. As part of the format of the *special* class, it was agreed that both men and women should lead the discussion. No one seemed to notice that the issue under discussion was automatically decided by the very format that was used to resolve the issue!

It was hardly surprising that, in the wake of the class, the elders announced that women would be permitted to teach mixed adult classes. Before any formal *proclamation*, the *transformation* had already taken place!

Overruling principle and precedent can also happen without any formal announcement whatever. One reason transformation is preferred over formal overruling is the matter of appearances. As far as I know, no congregation among the churches of Christ has changed its sign to read "The Cultural Church." No matter how desperately some want the churches of Christ to radically change, they are convinced that keeping up appearances is important. Therefore, they don't talk about overruling biblical precedent, they simply get on with doing things in radically different ways.

In this regard, one might consider the increasingly-popular "ministry teams" or "committee system" which in many congregations has replaced the normal functions of elders and deacons. Instead of fighting the battle over whether women (or single men or husbands without children) can be formally appointed as elders and deacons, an end-run is made that achieves the desired result without seeming to overturn obvious biblical instructions calling only those meeting certain qualifications to the special responsibility of congregational leadership.

In this and other instances, the method of overturning biblical authority is "to acknowledge, but ignore," or "to acknowledge, but sidestep." And the cultural church is particularly adept at this process, because it owes its first allegiance to the authority of conventional wisdom. For us, what could be more natural than the "committee system"? It's as American as baseball, apple pie, and Chevrolet! The surprise is not that culture deftly manages to circumvent biblical authority, but that biblical authority manages to still get honorable mention.

Turning Principle Into Rule

One of the most subtle ways of overturning principle is to chip away at it through inconsistent practical implementation until nothing is left but a fairly harmless rule. Many of those who say that they agree with the *principle* of male spiritual leadership, for example, are comfortable with men giving up their leadership responsibility at every point except (for some) when it comes to being elders, or (for others) elders and preachers. For them, anything else goes. In all other matters, the role of men and women is doctrinally indistinguishable.

Ironically, by ignoring specific biblical "rules" to the contrary, they find themselves left with more arbitrariness than the "rules" they are trying to avoid! All of a sudden, what was meant to be a pervasive principle of male spiritual leadership (both in the church and in the home) has become a legalistic classification meant only for church governance in which women are arbitrarily excluded from the very "top" positions.

Such reasoning illustrates once again how we can continue to pay lip-service to a principle while in practice having all but overruled it. In such a case, our hermeneutics is of no value whatsoever. What does it matter that we correctly determine biblical principles if we then allow ourselves to act inconsistently with what we discover to be God's leading?

Choosing From Among the Many Examples

When we turn to the task of determining the weight to be given to biblical examples, the problem we face is choosing which examples are merely coincidental occurrences and which are authoritative precedent. We must avoid at all cost any smorgasbord-like process in which the examples we whimsically choose to follow are authoritative while all others are thereby irrelevant.

Typically, we have four basic choices regarding biblical examples: 1) Accept both the practice and the principle (as in baptism); 2) Reject the practice, but retain the principle (as in footwashing); 3) Adapt a practice in order to preserve a principle (women wearing hats instead of veils); and 4) Reject both the practice and the principle because of some overriding reason (as with charismatic or "Pentecostal" gifts).

None of the four choices is easy. The first two choices encounter the problem of deciding when forms are culturally-based and when they are not. It is here that clearly-articulated principles become the backstop. Were it not for the attached principles, metaphors, and specific guidelines given to us in Scripture, even baptism might be suspect on this score. Ritual purification by immersion was already very much a part of the Jewish religious culture by the time of John the Baptist, Jesus, and the apostles. (That's why no one on Pentecost protested the call for baptism or had to inquire what it was.)

It was not baptism itself that was new, but baptism in the name of Jesus for the forgiveness of sins. That which previously was *culture-based* (ritual purification) became *transcultural* when appropriated as a faith-responsive act having unique Christian significance. Baptism became transcultural when Jesus gave it significance in his own baptism and in his commission to the apostles to go into all the world, teaching and baptizing *the nations.* It became transcultural when the apostles taught the importance of baptism to both Jewish and Gentile converts.

By contrast, another form of washing—footwashing— never made the transition from cultural form to doctrinal substance, and therefore is not to be taken as precedent. Whereas we see any number of *examples* of footwashing, we never encounter any *directives* mandating footwashing as part of Christian worship or living. Footwashing itself was never associated with any religious expression. Therefore, when footwashing *as a custom* ceased, so did any chance that it would become transcultural.

The *doctrinal* distinction between baptism and footwashing is typical of the approach we must take in our first two choices. Culture alone might produce the odd example; but culture backed by biblical teaching lifts the example out of the category of being *strictly cultural.*

How Important Is the Form?

Choice number three (reconstructing the example to fit our own purposes) can be both difficult and seductive. Deciding when a particular form is culturally-based and when it is not is often a thorny question. We tend to think that our modern circumstances are always more appropriate than more ancient forms as found in the Bible. Therefore, our initial instinct is to dismiss the *specific form* of the example, and content ourselves with implementing the spirit of the example in a different way. That works well only as long as the new form faithfully implements the principle involved.

For example, what difference does it make that we meet in modern church buildings rather than in synagogues as some of the early Christians did? (We don't worship "in the mountains or in Jerusalem, but in spirit and truth."[6]) Or what difference does it make that we use multiple cups for the fruit of the vine rather than the one cup with which Jesus initiated the Lord's Supper? (It was the contents, not the container, that he blessed as the "cup.")

Where we get into trouble is in violating the spirit of the example by changing its form—whether it be sprinkling instead of immersion, "priests" instead of "evangelists," or—if we are not careful about form and function—"ministry teams" instead of elders and deacons.

As to proper *form,* our best safeguard is usually the matter of repetition. In all the examples of baptism, immersion is always indicated, not sprinkling. By contrast, we have no multiple references to the "one cup" which might have indicated that having only one cup is important.

Making Wholesale Exceptions to Biblical Precedent

Choice number four is a kind of "fencing off" of certain types of activity from being recognized as precedent because of some overriding principle. These "exceptions from precedent" are consistent with what may be the "exceptional nature" of their use in the first place.

We must be careful, here, but it is somewhat like the rubric we have in law, that "When the reason for the rule ceases to exist, so ought the rule." (I say "careful," because it is easy to convince ourselves that we always know for certain when the reason for the rule no longer exists. The truth is that God may have his own reasons which we fail to fully appreciate.)

This "fencing off" process explains how we are able to justify disregarding such New Testament practices as prophecy, tongues, interpretation, healing, and, in some cases, laying on of hands—all of which certainly *look like* precedents. Were it not for some overriding reason indicating that exceptions are to be made in the case of spiritual gifts, we would be bound to practice them.

A more complete discussion of spiritual gifts and their applicability to the church today is outside the scope of this book. Suffice it to say that passages relating to spiritual gifts must surely be the prime example of the importance of *purpose* in our not-so-new hermeneutic.

After asking the exegetical questions of Who, What, When, Where, and Why, our fellowship has rejected the practice of these special gifts on the basis that they were given for a specific time and purpose which no longer exists.

Accordingly, we have determined that the numerous New Testament references to spiritual gifts are to be "fenced off" as exceptions to biblical precedent. (The renewed interest in spiritual gifts on the part of some in our fellowship will have to be met with a vigorous reexamination of our basic premise regarding the limited purpose of such gifts.)

On a much larger scale (also outside the scope of our immediate task in this book) is the "fencing off" of Old Testament examples from New Testament examples. Whereas we accept Old Testament examples as a source of still-valid godly principles, we do not follow them as specific precedent for Christian faith and worship.

Although we are not always terribly precise in distinguishing between the two testaments, the basic distinction has to do with what we know as *dispensations.* We take our direction from the teaching of Christ, not the laws of Moses. We are under the new dispensation, not the old. If something of the Mosaical law is carried over from one dispensation to the next, we follow it only because it has Christ's stamp of approval.

Where the "fencing off" of whole sections of Scripture legitimately takes place, it is important to note that it is done for reasons quite apart from any cultural considerations. If we've got it right, we make these exceptions from precedent on the basis of a correct understanding of Scripture, not on the basis of either church tradition or personal whims.

To that extent, we are not really making exceptions to precedent at all. What we are saying is that, for purely scriptural reasons, what may once have been precedent is no longer precedent.

Rising Above the Merely Human

As with any hermeneutic, *purpose, principle, and precedent* will require thoughtful and altogether humble attempts at making proper application. There is no magic wand, no scientific formula, no mystic secret that can give us total precision.

In that regard, I am sympathetic with those who urge us to seek a Christ-centered hermeneutic—to see Jesus as the grid through which all biblical understanding must pass.

How better to overcome the fallibility of our feeble interpretative enterprise than to stamp his image on book, chapter, and verse?

Yet what immediately catches our interest is the fact that Jesus himself demonstrated the use of more-than-familiar hermeneutics as he called upon principles and precedents to reason with his hearers and to support his claim of being the Son of God.

No better example of this is found than in Matthew 22 where Jesus engages the Sadducees in a dialogue about the Resurrection. The discussion ranges from *principles* inherent within the Levirate marriage law in Deuteronomy 25, to the *precedent* provided by the marital (or non-marital) status of angels. We even see Jesus sorting out the historical background of *purpose* in order to correctly apply to the Sadducees a statement which God had made to Moses. Rather than using *himself* as a hermeneutical approach to Scripture, Jesus did exactly what *we* do. He looked to "commands" and "examples"—to purpose, principle, and precedent.

The problem with saying that Jesus himself ought to be our hermeneutic is that we are inescapably left with the bias of our own *human* grid. It is not enough to ask, "Is this activity consistent with the person of Jesus?" Or, "Will Jesus be seen in us by others watching what we do?" Those questions simply beg the further question: Who is our Jesus? How do we see him? What kind of person do we want him to be?

Is our Jesus the compassionate, forgiving Jesus who told the adulterous woman to go away and sin no more?[7] Or is our Jesus the judgmental crusader indignantly overturning the merchants' tables in the Temple?[8] Do we want a Jesus meek and mild, or a Jesus who is Lord of the universe, assigning his enemies to the fires of hell?[9]

Before Jesus can be our hermeneutic, he must first pass through our own personally-chosen tinted glasses. The problem is that we can take *Jesus* out of context with as much ease as we can take a *verse* out of context. If we focus on only one facet of Jesus to the exclusion of others, we can miss the gospel story as surely as with any humanly-devised hermeneutic.

As a practical matter, Jesus simply cannot be the grid through which we filter every scripture. There are any number of concerns, especially about the work and worship of the church, which Jesus himself never addressed, not even as a matter of principle. Never do we know his mind regarding the qualifications for elders, or hear him speak about the handling of church finances. Not once are we given his thoughts on the music of the church or when we should meet in his name for worship.

And as much as we might pay lip service to Jesus being our ultimate hermeneutic, the plain fact is that there is a growing unwillingness to acknowledge what he *does address*, either in word or in deed, regarding such controversial issues as divorce or the role of women.

Certainly, a Christ-centered theology must always be our frame of reference, and forever remain our ultimate anchor point. But the "Jesus grid" is always held in human hands. Jesus himself foresaw the problem when he asked, "Who do people say the Son of Man is?"[10] A Christ-centered grid changes with each different answer to that question.

The Futility of Theological Hermeneutics

Attempts at a theological hermeneutic fall short for yet another reason. They inevitably end up with a theological dog chasing a hermeneutical tail. Granted, nothing could be more important than keeping Christ in the center of our theology. But we know absolutely nothing about Christ that is not in Scripture. So, if to get *to* Christ we must first go *through* Christ, then our search for Christ-centeredness becomes a vicious circle.

Put it another way. Without doubt, Christ (as *the Way*) is the "road" that we must stay on. But to say that we read the text with a Christ-centered hermeneutic is like saying we stay on the road by staying on the road!

The same idea goes for interpreting Scripture "through God, Christ, and the Holy Spirit," as others prefer to put it. If theologically we set God, Christ, and the Holy Spirit as our goal on a distant horizon, it is meaningless to turn around and say that we use God, Christ, and the Holy Spirit to chart our way to that goal. Consider the implications of such a statement: If we already have God, Christ, and the Holy Spirit available as our compass point, then God, Christ, and the Holy Spirit are no longer a distant goal. Using such an approach, that for which we seek is that which we already have!

Isn't the real concern whether or not we have a Christ-centered *theology*? A Christ-centered *faith*? A Christ-centered *life*? A Christ-centered *church*? Isn't that the message we want to take to the cultural church? Getting our theology and our hermeneutics mixed up is helping no one. At best, it only serves to distract us; at worst, it provides a subtle basis for unbridled subjectivism.

Appealing to the Holy Spirit

If the "Jesus grid" itself is vulnerable to human interpretation, is there any possible way to remove ourselves from the picture and let God truly lead us? Many people today think so. An increasing number among our fellowship are convinced that our best hermeneutic is not any articulated method of interpretation but the working of the Holy Spirit.

In turning to the Holy Spirit, there is both danger and promise. The danger is obvious. Just as we can see Jesus as we *want* to see him, we can also hear the Holy Spirit as we *want* to hear him. Everywhere I go among the larger "Christian community," I hear people attributing their spiritual assurance to the leading of the Holy Spirit. As often as not, where the Holy Spirit is leading them is directly contrary to what the Holy Spirit guided holy men of old to write by way of Scripture.

Even in the church today, I hear appeals to the leading of the Holy Spirit as justification for doing that which the Bible plainly forbids. It's just too easy to let the Holy Spirit pass across our lips as a mantra to verify whatever it is that we want to do. When abused, appealing to the Holy Spirit can be the ultimate pseudo-spiritual self-justification.

If one wants to see just how far off the path of biblical practice one can get by misunderstanding "the leading of the Holy Spirit," one need only look at the Friends Church. The Quakers had their roots in what was known as the Radical

Reformation, whose leaders affirmed that "the Living Spirit is the final authority, not the Bible." Proceeding from that fundamental assumption, the Quakers spiritualized away both baptism and the Lord's Supper, and still today practice neither.

Such a radical departure from Scripture suggests trouble even from the very start when we begin to modify biblical practices because of what we perceive to be "the leading of the Spirit."

First and foremost, we must acknowledge that the Holy Spirit tells us nothing more than "that which is written." No one gets a special, personal revelation from God revealing any previously-unrevealed truth. It is in that sense that early restorationists adamantly (and correctly) insisted that the revelatory work of the Holy Spirit was limited to the sacred page of Scripture.

Any other view of revelation risks the danger of our going *beyond* that which is written. Any other view conveniently allows us to pull the Holy Spirit out of our pocket or purse for whatever amendments to Scripture we might wish to make.

But there is promise as well as danger. Surely by now we have come to accept the providential working of the Holy Spirit in our lives as the promised gift of which Peter spoke on Pentecost.[11] Surely we acknowledge—and hopefully experience—the living presence of God's Spirit among us. Even *within* us![12]

If the Word of God is "the sword of the Spirit," it is nevertheless, as the writer of Hebrews assures us, a revelation that is both *living* and *active*. "Sharper than any double-edged sword, it penetrates even to dividing soul and spirit, joints and marrow; it judges the thoughts and attitudes of the heart."[13]

But if it is not for the further revelation of truth, then to what end? Is it not to open our minds to *receive* God's truth?[14] Is it not for the *discernment* of that truth which has already been revealed?[15] Is it not for the *strength* to apply in our lives what we learn from Scripture to be the will of God?[16]

I, for one, believe that the Holy Spirit moves in my life in all of those ways. If ever I am able to transcend my own human rationality, it is because of the power of the Holy Spirit working through me. I can't do it on my own.

That is where prayer comes into the picture. The irony is that, in praying for insight, I need the Holy Spirit even to know how to pray! But thank God for his promise:

> The Spirit helps us in our weakness. We do not know what we ought to pray for, but the Spirit himself intercedes for us with groans that words cannot express.[17]

In my case, shamefully, I confess that I am passively dragged kicking and screaming into His presence far more than I actively invoke His presence through prayer. I'm better at talking about "prayerful study" than I am at actually doing it. While it is always my desire and aim, it is not always my literal daily prayer.

For that reason, *purpose, principle, and precedent* ought really to be purpose, principle, precedent, and *prayer*—just as a constant reminder of our human limitations and of the divine resource which we have in the Person of the Holy Spirit for leading us more clearly into God's truth.

The Hermeneutic of Trust

As we close our thoughts on how to apply *purpose, principle, and precedent,* we would do well to consider the opening verses of Hebrews:

> In the past God spoke to our forefathers through the prophets at many times and in various ways, but in these last days he has spoken to us by his Son, whom he appointed heir of all things, and through whom he made the universe.[18]

In the past, God has not always spoken in the same way to his people. Sometimes he has spoken through the law and the prophets; sometimes through tongues, prophecies, and interpretation. Knowing how he speaks to us today is what hermeneutics is all about.   More importantly, *believing* that he speaks to us today is what *faith* is all about.

Surely that is the key. If we don't trust that God is still speaking to us today through his Word, then our search for a helpful hermeneutic is wasted effort. The most important question for the cultural church is not, Are we understanding the Bible correctly? The most important question is, Have we given up on the notion that God is still speaking to us?

If we truly believe that God has something to tell us, then we must trust that, indeed, *God has spoken*, and that, therefore, he will make his message known to those who sincerely seek him—even despite our hopeless hermeneutics, if necessary!

THIRTEEN

The Deafening Roar of Biblical Silence

Cast away authority, and authority shall forsake you!
— Robert H. Benson

Who ever would have believed that we would once again be hearing calls for instrumental music in the worship of the church? Of course, it's only a trickle now, but the direction we're headed is easy to see from all the *background vocal imitation* of musical instruments by our more contemporary singing groups. In a pop-and-rock-music-oriented generation, what else might we expect?

Call me out-of-touch, but I am a rock solid believer in *a cappella* singing. When it comes to worship, I despise pianos and, for the most part, loathe organs. Don't even talk to me about a trombone, synthesizer, or drum! They all disturb me, and—to a greater or lesser extent—they all get in my way of communicating with God through my own singing.

On the other hand, even as I write these words, in the background I hear the stirring sounds of one of my favorite tapes: "Hymns Triumphant," by London's National Philharmonic Orchestra and the Amen Choir. My little stone cottage resonates as I am transcended by lofty *hymns* of faith while I struggle to write some simple *book* of faith. Somehow, I feel a greater Presence through the music. It calls me onward and lifts me higher. What can possibly match the Amen Choir's majestic presentation of "To God Be the Glory"?

In sorting out the mixed feelings I have about instrumental music, I must say that the transcendence I feel when I hear it in other contexts is matched only by my abhorrence of it when it is a part of congregational worship. This contradiction springs from a combination of aesthetic appreciation (which outside the worship greatly favors it) and doctrinal concern (which calls me to reject it).

I share these conflicting reflections on singing and instrumental music to set the scene for a discussion we are forced to have in a book on how we are to understand the Bible. Church music points us to the more fundamental issue of the authority of Scripture and how it is to be applied. In particular, it highlights the authority of scriptural *silence*.

Freedom Where Silence

On September 7, 1809, Thomas Campbell read aloud his landmark restorationist statement, the well-known "Declaration and Address." In his opening remarks before reading the Declaration, Campbell used an expression that has been traced back as far as the 1500's. His pronouncement that day, "We speak where the Bible speaks, and are silent where the Bible is silent," has been repeated as a restorationist rubric ever since.

The second half of that rubric, *"silent where the Bible is silent,"* has two seemingly-contradictory, yet entirely-consistent implications. The first implication was Campbell's response to the human innovation that had been added to Scripture over centuries of church tradition, as embodied in denominationalism. The genius of the restoration perspective was its recognition that we are bound by Scripture when it *speaks*, but are not bound when it is *silent*. Or, to put it another way, we are bound by Scripture, but not bound by anything outside of Scripture.

Where the Bible does *not* speak, no person, no church, nor any creed has a right to impose further doctrine or tradition on anyone. Paul reminds us, "It is for freedom that Christ has set us free."[1] As if directly addressing the imposition of human tradition in Christian worship, Paul continues, "Stand firm, then, and do not let yourselves be burdened again by a yoke of slavery."

The Authority of Silence

The second implication that flows from Thomas Campbell's statement (one which Campbell himself recognized, although with caution) is the authority of Scripture which comes through any *intended* silence. Silence, when specifically intended, can be as guiding and authoritative as any other form of expression. In this sense, "We speak where the Bible speaks," because it is God's authoritative *Word.* We are "silent where the Bible is silent," because it is God's authoritative *Silence.* Given the proper context and purpose, what God *doesn't* tell us can be as important as what he *does* tell us.

Whenever any document is held to be authoritative, respect for its silence *must* exist, otherwise why consider the text authoritative? If a document is not honored in its silence, it is a different document—a new document formed by human fabrication and innovation where we ourselves "fill in the blanks" of that which is *not* said. In the end, the amended document no longer looks like the original one, even if we continue to pay it lip service.

We see the principle of silence at work in the specific instructions given to the Israelites pertaining to their worship. Because God specifically called for animal sacrifices, special feasts, and tithing, for example, the Israelites correctly understood that they were not free to introduce other forms of worship. Walking on hot coals to the glory of God might indeed have been an act of humble contrition, but it would not have reflected God's will regarding tabernacle worship.

If we think that the restoration movement invented the authority of silence, we're wrong. In fact, the authority of silence couldn't be more biblical. What can be more instructive than when the people of Israel were told not to take away or *add to* the laws given to Moses?[2] When rebuking the Corinthians for their pride and divisiveness, Paul referred to the same idea: "Do not go beyond what is written."[3]

Lessons From the Law

At the risk of automatically being associated with legalism, or being accused of pushing the Bible as a *constitution*, I would also point us to the ongoing struggle over judicial interpretation of our own U. S. Constitution as it relates to the authority of silence.

Reducing the battle among constitutional law experts to its simplest form, those who are "strict constructionists" use the argument from silence to say that the words of the Framers are always the outer limits of Constitutional authority. Court "liberals" reject the argument from silence, saying that the Supreme Court has a duty to "read into" the Constitution whatever would keep it alive for a twentieth-century nation very much different from America in the late eighteenth century. (We've heard this before. It's "their story" versus "our story.")

The battle is not simply one of legal theory. How we view the silence of the Constitution has tremendous practical consequences. Most notably, since 1973 when the Supreme Court decided *Roe v. Wade*, the nation has been in a virtual civil war over the legalization of abortion. *Roe v. Wade* limited attempts by individual states to criminalize abortion, saying that abortion is part of a woman's Constitutionally-guaranteed "right of privacy." The obvious problem with that ruling was its reliance on a "privacy right" which is never specifically mentioned in the Constitution.

Interestingly, Justice Blackmun's opinion in *Roe* used a line of reasoning similar to "necessary inference." He said that if there is a right of sexual privacy for married couples (which the Court had already recognized), then, by inference, the right to have an abortion should necessarily follow. Of course, one might (and should) question whether such an inference was truly "necessary," or even logical, but Justice Blackmun saw it as a way of *getting around* Constitutional silence, rather than being *restricted* by it. (Caution to us, indeed, in the *selective use of inference*—whether in support or derogation of biblical silence.)

At some future time, the Supreme Court may reject Justice Blackmun's "inference" and overturn *Roe v. Wade*.

But what this case so well demonstrates is the wide gap between those who see biblical silence as a red light, and those who see it as a green light.

Of course, the issue is never as clear-cut as that. "Strict constructionists," whether in law or in religion, are not always *that strict*. Even conservative jurists agreed, for example, that although it was not mentioned specifically in the Constitution, there is a right of sexual privacy for married couples. All agree that it falls within what lawyers call the "penumbra" (or "aura") of the Constitution, and is so fundamental that it *must* be a right.

In the realm of biblical interpretation, "strict constructionists," who otherwise would honor the silence of Scripture, rarely object to church buildings, song books, or four-part harmony, even though none of those are *specifically authorized*, or even mentioned, in the Bible. Those things are considered to be so incidental to other clear objectives that they *must* be a right. But how are we to know? And in what way do song books and four-part harmony differ from musical instruments?

Our most challenging difficulty in implementing the authority of silence is in knowing when biblical silence was intended to convey God's final word. We can see the problem of interpreting silence elsewhere. Take, for example, the silence of one who is accused of a crime. Should his silence be admissible at his trial, thereby permitting the jury to infer his guilt? (Surely, an innocent man would vehemently deny his guilt, wouldn't he?)

But what if, at the time of his alleged silence, he had not yet been confronted with a criminal charge? Would his silence have any possible meaning other than coincidence? Even after confrontation, a prisoner might well remain silent because he's been told that he has a Constitutional *right* to remain silent.

In a similar fashion, then, we must be careful to sort out when biblical silence is significant and when it is not. And that invariably leads us right back to the *purpose* for which the text was originally intended. As much as anything, the authority of silence is a matter of being faithful to the text *according to its original purpose.*

Silence Works Only If Intended

Turning again to the law as an example, suppose we had a particular piece of legislation relating to the state's sales tax. It says nothing about income tax or property tax. Now suppose that a farmer were to point to the silence of the statute as support for his contention that he was exempt from paying *property* tax. The judge would be justified in throwing the farmer out of court on his ear! Since the law addresses only *sales* tax, we know nothing one way or the other about any exemptions from the *property* tax. Therefore, it would be improper to draw *any* inferences from the silence of the sales-tax statute.

But now suppose, on the other hand, that the statute *did* apply to property tax and said specifically, "The following persons are exempt from paying property tax: widows and widowers, the handicapped, veterans, and city employees." In this case, we would know for sure that the legislature specifically intended its silence beyond the listed exemptions to be controlling. There's no question. The farmer is not among those who are specifically listed as being exempt.

If the farmer were to say, "But the statute nowhere specifically says that farmers are *not* exempt," again the farmer wouldn't get the slightest hearing. What the statute *did* say was meant to exclude anything that it *didn't* say. Any other result would create a greater respect for what the law *omitted* than for what it *stated*. Whatever more legitimate purpose it may serve, the authority of silence must never be used in such a way as to permit the unscrupulous to engage in "loophole theology."

The point is that the effect of "silence," whether in law or in Scripture, rests in the stated or clear *purpose* of the text. Before making an argument based on the silence of Scripture, therefore, we must 1) first make sure that the particular passage addresses the particular question being asked, and 2) determine whether the passage intends its silence to be prohibitive of any other practice.

This principle of silence may be applied to specific passages, or to whole documents, such as the entirety of the New

Testament. And that brings us back to church music and the authority of silence. No New Testament passage specifically addresses the issue of instrumental music. We know from a number of passages that first-century Christians sang as part of their mutual worship together, but there is no mention of instruments such as were used in the time of David.

What are the implications of this textual silence regarding instruments? Was it an *intended* silence, or was it merely *coincidental*? Does New Testament silence regarding musical instruments give us a red light or a green light?

Why Was There Silence Regarding Instruments?

By concentrating on the silence of certain individual passages, sometimes we tend to forget that there is a more wide-sweeping argument from silence that we simply take for granted, probably because—on any other matter of doctrine—it's so obvious that few people would take issue with it. I refer to the striking difference between Old Testament worship and New Testament worship.

Hardly anyone today would suggest that Christian worship ought to include the Feast of Weeks, the Day of Atonement, or the Year of Jubilee. No one is pressing for purification after childbirth, or Nazirite vows, or isolation following diagnosis of the itch. Yet these are all very much a part of the laws of Moses, given by God to the nation of Israel for their observance.

When we turn to the New Testament, we find none of these practices in first-century worship. There is virtually unanimous agreement that they are not a part of Christian worship and faithfulness. Why? Because, as the apostles repeatedly point out, they are part of a worship system that was done away with under Christ.

The writer of Hebrews, in particular, stresses the superiority of Christ over the ritual worship which had been given to the nation of Israel. In Christ, there would no longer be temple or tabernacle,[4] or the Levitical priesthood,[5] or animal sacrifices,[6] or any of the other practices associated with Jewish worship. Unless a given expression of worship (like singing or praying) was specifically carried over into Christian worship, it was eliminated as part of the old covenant which was made obsolete by the new covenant in Christ.[7]

Therefore, New Testament silence about temple-worship practices is not coincidental. It is specifically explained. It is intentional. When the Hebrew writer insisted that we are now under a better covenant, he could well have listed the former Jewish practices one by one and reiterated their obsolescence under Christ. Had he done so, instrumental music undoubtedly would have been on the list as surely as tithing, circumcision, and kosher food.

The desire of many Jewish Christians to retain circumcision, in particular, as part of Christian observance simply underscored their misunderstanding about the radical difference between Jewish observance and Christian worship. It was a complete switch. One system replaced another. Certainly, eternal spiritual truths remained the same. But, in terms of worship ritual, Christianity supplanted Judaism lock, stock, and barrel, "bag and baggage."

In a way, New Testament silence regarding instruments shouldn't be all that surprising. Many people today forget that no instruments ever accompanied singing under *Mosaic* worship. (The silver trumpet was merely a signal horn.) It wasn't until the time of King David that musical instruments were used as part of temple worship by the people of Israel. At that time, of course, a number of instruments were introduced, including David's harp and the various "stringed instruments," tambourines, flutes, and trumpets.[8] Among the Levites, 4,000 were specially chosen to praise the Lord with instruments.[9]

A significant historical footnote suggests that even the Jews did not count musical instruments to be either mandatory or central to Jewish worship. The fact that instruments were not used in the Jewish synagogue during the intertestamental period and on into the first century indicates a return to the pre-Davidic form of worship in which no instruments were used in the congregational worship of Israel.

The important thing to remember is that musical instruments, whether considered to be of Moses or of David, were never mentioned as part of Christian worship. Assuming (as we must) that the purpose of the New Testament is to be our exclusive guide to Christian practice, one can only conclude from the remarkable silence regarding instrumental music that the instruments added to Jewish worship during the time of King David were part of a pre-Christian system that was swept away at the foot of the cross.

To whatever extent musical instruments in temple worship may have been countenanced or even commanded by God, they, like other rituals of temple worship, would have been but a "type" of Christian worship, the "anti-type." Just as we now are the "temple" of God, and offer up sacrifices of praise (as opposed to animal sacrifices), so too our voices need no embellishment. The change from Jewish to Christian worship was like night and day. If the substance of faith, praise, and adoration remained, the form of its expression changed dramatically.

Verifying the Intent of Textual Silence

In contrast to the many Old Testament passages referring to musical instruments in temple worship, in the New Testament text not one sound of a musical instrument is heard—not a trumpet, not a harp, not the quietest jingle of a tambourine! Singing, yes. Musical instruments, no. Relative to musical instruments, there is only an ominous, haunting silence.

But how can we be sure that the textual silence was intended? Could it have been merely circumstantial? Is it possible that New Testament Christians actually used instruments even though the text does not refer to their use?

Naturally, what the church did in the post-New Testament centuries is not always a safe guide to Christian doctrine, because we know that much of what it did became unbiblical. But the history of the early church confirms that instruments were the exception rather than the rule in early Christian worship, and that later use of instruments was both an innovation and a radical departure from New Testament worship.

Just as circumcision was a hold-over practice among some of the Jewish Christians, apparently there was also scattered use of instruments in the earliest Christian centuries (especially the lyre in accompaniment of the psalms).

But there is no evidence of widespread, acceptable usage of instruments in Christian worship. Most early church writers disapproved of instrumental music, citing among other reasons its association with pagan worship.

Significantly, it was not until the seventh century (at the very earliest) that there was a move toward inclusion of the organ in the worship of the Roman Catholic Church. Even then, the organ was only given to the people as "a concession." From the *Catholic Encyclopedia* comes this important acknowledgement: "Pius X, in his '*motu proprio*' on church music (22 November 1903) in paragraph IV, says, 'Although the music *proper to the Church* is purely vocal music, music with the accompaniment of the organ is also *permitted* [my emphasis]."[10]

Not until the last 30 years has there been any official pronouncement giving the organ formal approval. Hardly surprising in the wake of centuries of unofficial "permission" for the organ's use, we now have the 1963 pronouncement of Vatican II's liturgical constitution (paragraph 120) saying that the pipe organ is held in "high esteem." But it was not always so.

If you ever tour the Sistine Chapel at the Vatican, you may notice that there is no organ as you might expect to find in other Catholic chapels or cathedrals. Of course, it is now primarily a museum and no longer regularly used as a chapel, but the point is that no organ was ever installed. The non-instrumental status of the Sistine Chapel reflects the historical view of the church which, until our own generation, officially frowned on the use of instruments.

As we witness the apparent demise of communism, how can we escape noticing what we are freely being shown about worship in the heart of the former Soviet Union? For all its deviations from the first-century pattern, you'll still find few, if any, instruments in the Russian Orthodox Church with its millions of adherents. Nor in the Eastern Orthodox Church, with its own millions.

In fact, the only place you'll find musical instruments in unquestioned official use (Roman Catholic sanction being somewhat in doubt over the centuries) is in Protestant denominations, *whose founders and leaders almost uniformly rejected the instrument.* I only wish there were pages enough to give you quote upon quote from such Protestant Reformers as John Calvin, John Knox, Ulric Zwingli, and Cotton Mather. (Martin Luther was a notable exception.) For them, the organ was "an ensign of Baal," and "the idol of the Philistines!"

As far as church history is concerned, the most telling confirmation of textual silence, ironically, is found in the very words, *a cappella*. *Cappella* is Latin for *chapel* or *church*. Taken in its literal meaning, the Italian *a cappella* means "in chapel style," or "in the style of the church." From the first century onward, vocal music was so distinctive from the instrumental music used in both pagan worship and private entertainment that it was uniquely known as music *of the church*—that is, *a cappella!* So when we say that we sing *a cappella*, we are affirming what millions of believers over the centuries have affirmed—that the music *of the church* is distinctively *vocal!*

What all of this church history tells us is that New Testament silence regarding instruments in Christian worship was not coincidental, but intentional. Unlike the Jews in their temple worship, Christians did not accompany their singing with instruments. Musical instruments were as foreign to Christian worship as were animal sacrifices and the Day of Atonement. And it was for the same reason: musical instruments were associated with a system of ritual that was replaced by a revolutionary form of worship in the Kingdom of Christ.

The silence of first-century-and-beyond *practice* confirms the silence of New Testament *text*. With the intent of the silence having thus been established through Scripture and confirmed through history, we have no warrant for using musical instruments in Christian worship. The intended silence of the text is as instructive as if we had a passage of Scripture telling us straight out: "Musical instruments are not to be used as part of Christian worship." It's one of those classic cases where silence speaks volumes.

What's So Special About Singing?

In outlining for us a revolutionary, Christ-oriented form of faith and worship, the New Testament clearly teaches that first-century Christians practiced a radically different form of worship. For the most part, Christian worship was "internalized," being stripped of all external *physical* trappings, whether it be a physical tabernacle, the ark of the Lord, or the centrality of Jerusalem as the designated place of worship. The only apparent exceptions to this rule were the physical *bread* and *wine* of the Lord's Supper and the physical *water* of baptism.

That may well explain why the music of the church is *a cappella*. Carefully examine the context of the passages which deal with singing as an expression of Christian worship and you quickly discover how closely singing is linked with the "internal."

In both Ephesians 5:19 and Colossians 3:16, Paul is talking about the believer's Christian walk—whether expressed individually or as a body. In his letter to the Ephesians, for example, Paul is encouraging them (and us) to no longer walk in darkness and sin, but in the light of Christ.[11]

"Be very careful, then, how you live—not as unwise but as wise," says Paul. "Do not get drunk on wine, which leads to debauchery. Instead, be filled with the Spirit. Speak to one another with psalms, hymns and spiritual songs. Sing and make music in your heart to the Lord, always giving thanks to God the Father for everything, in the name of our Lord Jesus Christ."

Whatever else it may say, Ephesians chapter five is primarily an exhortation for us to live Spirit-filled lives. For Paul, it's all the difference between "spirits"—as in "*wine* and *spirits*"—and the *Holy Spirit*. Instead of our being able to sing only when we get drunk (as is the case with many people in the world who seek artificial happiness out of a bottle), we are to be so filled with the Spirit that our overflowing joy just naturally expresses itself in song!

I can't begin to tell you how I love Paul's contrast between what amounts to some debauched drunk out on the street at 2:00 in the morning, singing at the top of his lungs, and the completely sober spontaneity of my own singing, first welling up from sheer inner joy, then bursting out in the form of some spiritual song!

And that's just here in my little English cottage with no one else around! It's all the more meaningful when I can join in singing with fellow Christians during our time of worship together. When we join our voices and (more importantly) our souls together in song, four-part harmony has little to do with "four-part," and everything to do with "harmony!"

Also notice that singing is to be reflective of the inner person's focus—singing and "making music *in your heart* to the Lord." The most important music we are to make is neither instrumental *nor* vocal!

To be sure, our mutual joy will lead us to joint participation in "speaking to one another with psalms, hymns and spiritual songs." But it is not the outer expression of song that directly concerns Paul in this context. Rather, it is the inner expression of the heart before God.

It's the kind of singing that always brings tears to my eyes: the singing of those Christians who by virtue of physical disability *can't* sing, who *sign* their praises to God rather than *sing* them. It doesn't matter that there's no melody to be heard. God hears the song in their hearts!

Paul's letter to the Colossians brings us once again to the essence of singing.[12] "Since, then, you have been raised with Christ, set your hearts on things above...," Paul begins in chapter 3. "Put to death, therefore, whatever belongs to your earthly nature...," he continues. "As God's chosen people, holy and dearly loved, clothe yourselves with compassion, kindness, humility, gentleness, and patience." [And here comes the connection with singing.] "Let the peace of Christ rule in your hearts....And be thankful. Let the word of Christ dwell in you richly as you teach and admonish one another with all wisdom, and as you sing psalms, hymns, and spiritual songs with gratitude in your hearts to God."

Singing as a form of Christian worship is one of the special ways in which we invite Christ's Word to dwell within us. More than any emotion that musical orchestration might evoke, Christian singing is the call of the gospel moving to the beat of our hearts; the divine lyric set to the music of the soul. What instrument could ever improve on the melody of the message?[13]

Shutting Our Ears to the Silence

One could hope that current discussion of church music was prompted only by questions pertaining to hermeneutics, biblical authority, and the silence of the Scriptures. But there are increasing indications that what really is involved is the cultural church wanting to be like everyone else. Wanting to move from the traditional to the trendy. Wanting to rev up the decibels and entertain the crowds. Wanting to be spirit-*moved* even if not Spirit-*filled.*

Ironically, in our mad rush to cross over to the other side of the tracks and be more respectfully "mainstream," we overlook the fact that, when we sing without instruments, we *already are* among the vast majority of those who through history have found instrumental music to be unbiblical!

Those who use musical instruments, although far more noticeable in our own culture, are, in fact, the ones who are out of step with Christendom historically. Given both the silence of the New Testament and the resounding silence of history, the churches of Christ have been more "mainstream" than the "mainstream" all along. (Not that being "mainstream" matters in the least.)

Perhaps the most interesting thought of all is that, when other fellowships came to their respective understandings of the silence of Scripture on instrumental music, it was not through the alleged rationalistic, legalistic, "scientific method" of churches-of-Christ hermeneutics! The authority of biblical silence has been appreciated even by those far beyond our fellowship whenever they, too, have been willing to leave human innovation behind and submit themselves to divine authority.

And that, of course, is the reason why this chapter has been made necessary in a book about how to understand the Bible. The issue of instrumental music is simply one of the most graphic ways to reinforce the importance of respecting the silence of Scripture in *all* areas of faith and worship where a pattern has been established.

Whether or not the specific issue is church music, the question for each of us remains. In ignoring the sounds of silence, are we hearing from the Bible only what we want to hear? If so, why bother at all with Scripture—either in the quiet whisper of its plain teaching, or in the deafening roar of its silence?

FOURTEEN

Cultural Church, Or Church In Culture?

Tradition is the living faith of those now dead; traditionalism is the dead faith of those still living.
—Jaroslav Pelikan

These words are being written at the end of one of the most exhilarating and uplifting days that I have ever experienced in the body of Christ. For a week now, I have had the wonderful privilege of being in the City of Jerusalem where a small group of Christians and I have joined together in tracing the life of Jesus during his last week before the cross. Today, we spent the entire day, from morning to night, in fellowship and worship with brothers and sisters in the faith—Jewish believers who, like us, call on Jesus as Messiah.

Our worship together couldn't have been more different from the kind of worship services to which most of us are accustomed. (I had a feeling that something might be different from the moment I spied a 9 mm automatic pistol tucked into the waistband of a skirt worn by one of the young sisters who is an officer in the Israeli army!)

Just try to imagine a congregation of 50 or so believers, with people wandering in and out of the large upper-story meeting room as informally as if they were visiting in someone's home; the men wearing prayer shawls and yarmulkes; the reading of the Law from the Torah scroll (I had previously only seen pictures); responsive readings breaking into song and back again into readings; the speaker being interrupted with questions and comments; and times of vigorous debate over the meaning of Scripture.

I was particularly impressed with the respect and position shown to the eldest member of the congregation, a 75-year-old death-camp survivor by the name of Joseph. His poignant readings and singing of the psalms made my eyes water time and again. Without any official recognition or appointment, Joseph gave new meaning to the vital role of those who, by virtue of age and insight, are "elders" within the church.

Through it all, as in our own assemblies, there was preaching, praying, singing, and the Lord's Supper. The singing was not our customary four-part harmony, but traditional Jewish melodies. No formal collection was taken as part of the worship. A wooden box on the wall was used by the members of the congregation to deposit contributions for the ongoing work of the church.

And who could help but notice the mixture of ethnic backgrounds and languages? As an immigrant nation, Israel had attracted believers from former Soviet-bloc countries, from America, Bulgaria, and from within Israel itself. Even local Arabs (formerly Muslims) were included.

The many languages being spoken became a linguistic melting pot. There was Hebrew, of course, and Russian and Finnish. And, fortunately for us, there were many believers who spoke English. Being no more than two or three miles from the site of the old Temple, I couldn't help but think of that first-century Pentecost, when, by the power of the Holy Spirit, "each one heard them speaking in his own language."[1] On this occasion, we were at the mercy of human translators and the aid of radio technology to carry the message to remote headsets throughout the room.

Perhaps the most striking difference was the fact that we were meeting for worship on a Saturday night. But this had nothing to do with any trendy accommodation of those who might prefer to meet sometime other than the first day of the week. By Jewish reckoning, this *was* the first day of the week! When the sun had gone down on a bitter cold Sabbath day, we bowed together in prayer and partook of the bread and fruit of the vine—just as Jewish believers have done since the church began in the first century.

I only wish I could convey to you the vibrancy, joy, sincerity, and love with which we worshipped together on this most special day. Whether Jew or Gentile, I don't think any of us will ever forget it.

Christ in Culture

The body of Christ in Israel is not altogether unique in one respect. Over the years, I have been blessed to meet with Christians all around the world, and wherever there is a local, culturally-indigenous congregation, there will be noticeable differences in the form of worship. (Only "military congregations" seem to transplant "American" churches of Christ—lock, stock and barrel—to foreign soil.)

I think of Dublin, Ireland, and any number of other cities around the globe, which have only one formal service on Sunday. What we tend to take for granted—the ease of transportation—is simply not a luxury afforded to fellow Christians elsewhere. When getting to and from a place of worship can be an all-day affair, one time of worship (typically longer than ours) makes perfectly good sense.

I also think of congregation after congregation—usually small by our standards—which use only one or two cups for the fruit of the vine. They are not "one-cuppers" in any theological sense. It's just that one cup usually suffices for their need. And rarely do I hear an "invitation song." Or see ushers. Or find Wednesday night services (although normally there are Bible studies from house to house during the week.)

The point is that God calls the church to be *in culture* but not *of culture*. "In the world, but not of the world."[2] As long as there is respect for the leading of Scripture—in its purpose, principle, and precedent—the outer trappings may be as different as Joplin and Jerusalem, Billings and Bombay, Minneapolis and Moscow. Even as different as Nashville and New Orleans, Searcy and Syracuse, Temple Terrace and Toledo.

If we truly believe in congregational autonomy as we say we do, then we must honor the fact that we don't all speak the same language, wear the same clothes, drive the same automobiles, or implement the one biblical pattern in exactly the same way. Scripture after scripture reminds us that God calls us in diversity as well as in unity—or, perhaps it should be said, in unity *because of our very diversity.*

It should go without saying (but unfortunately doesn't) that cultural diversity doesn't give free license to ignore well-established biblical principle and precedent. Principle and precedent must always be the bottom line. But nothing could be clearer from Paul's epistles than the acceptability of both Jewish Christian worship and Gentile Christian worship, both highly ceremonial worship and worship reflecting a minimum of ritual.

Traditional or Trendy?

In relating to culture, the tendency for all of us is to slide inexorably to one extreme or the other. Seemingly, our only options are being *traditional* (holding on desperately to past culture) or *trendy* (grabbing on desperately to current culture). It's either, "We've always done it this way" (and so we're not about to change), or "we've never done it this way" (so why not try it?). Both approaches can kill the church—the former out of failure to respond to cultural change; the latter out of being vulnerable to every faddish idea that comes down the pike.

In a time of identity crisis such as ours, the tendency is toward the trendy. Mortified by the deadness of cold traditionalism, we run as fast as we can into the inviting arms of whatever the latest worship fad may be—whether raising our hands, or kneeling when in prayer, or huddling up in small groups for communion.

Does it strike you odd that I should include these worship forms as being "trendy"? What could be more ancient, you say, than the practice of raising holy hands or kneeling in prayer? And, of course, you are right. But why, then, are we not equally eager to return to such first-century practices as the laying on of hands, or widows being enrolled for support, or fasting? The inconsistent smorgasbord of biblical selectivity is not exclusively a characteristic of the "old hermeneutic." Hardly anything is more whimsically selective than shallow trendiness in worship.

The question is not whether it's biblical to get down on our knees when we pray (Of course it's biblical!), but whether we are also humbling ourselves before God's divine authority as we find it revealed in Scripture. Are there those in the church today who delight in raising holy hands while ignoring plain biblical teaching about other, more significant matters of worship? (And is there also some reason why raising hands is far more popular than actually getting down on our knees?)

Someone has suggested that what being non-denominational usually means to us is simply being ten years behind the denominations. How true! Remember when we bought everyone else's *used* "Joy Buses"? And do you not find it interesting that we are only now beginning to raise our hands during praise songs and to punctuate the worship with clapping?

As one who uncomfortably finds himself in the midst of other fellowships on frequent occasions, I must share with you the other striking implication of the ten-year time lag between us and the denominational world. Just look around and see where our trendiness is likely to lead us. In the churches around us, "more meaningful worship services" have already evolved into thinly-disguised entertainment. (Some among their own circles are now beginning to openly lament the almost-unnoticed transition from sacred to secular.) It started innocently enough with choruses, solos, and music ministry teams, then became the focal point in which worship leaders (particularly music leaders) stole the show and left the audience applauding the weekly worship "concert." Is that where we really want to go?

The novelty of trendy worship practices can be as self-deluding as any traditionalism ever was. Before we initiate something new, simply for the sake of change, we must ask ourselves whether we are breathing life into our worship to God, or merely following the crowd hoping to catch some of the excitement which faddishness tends to offer.

First-Century Timing Was No Accident

We might also do well to remind ourselves that God chooses his own timing. It was no coincidence that God established his kingdom at the exact historical moment of the first century—initially in a predominantly Jewish culture, and then in a Gentile culture more nearly like our own. Form and substance are not as easily divorced from each other as we sometimes like to think. Certainly, first-century culture was in many respects the culture of pagans. But in other respects (owing to the history of God's chosen people) it was the direct result of an interactive God—the same God who has always penetrated the larger culture of our humanity *at just the right time* in order to reveal the mystery of godliness. If we are tempted to toss the New Testament pattern into the trash basket simply because it reflects a culture other than our own, we are likely to miss the point altogether.

If, for example, the notion of elders seems a bit patriarchal for our time, and the idea of "shepherds" somewhat more pastoral than the urban scene in which most of us function from day to day, we must be careful not to immediately assume that the role of our spiritual leaders has radically changed.

I recently heard a series of "Shepherds' Talks" in which the role of elders was variously described as "mediators," "arbitrators," "encouragers," and "traffic cops." No mention whatever was made about *feeding* the flock or *leading* it—the two things that most aptly describe what shepherds do.

Nor does the increasingly popular idea of having elders serve for a two- or three-year term match the metaphor of a "shepherd." Such a view of "shepherds" is almost as incongruous as being appointed as a *father* for a set term! Are we sure that we are not reflecting current culture's corporate leadership structure in a way God never intended for those whom he has called through the metaphor of a "shepherd" to feed and lead his sheep?

On this point I enthusiastically join with those who are calling for greater attention to metaphors. But that's *biblical* metaphors, not metaphors of our own choosing. Change the metaphor and you change the meaning. Change the metaphor and you might not end up with the same "dynamic equivalent" after all.

The culture of Bible times must not be automatically dismissed as historically passe'. We must believe that the old, old story was told from a first-century perspective for a specific reason. Not only did it have to fit the initial recipients *first*, but it was also a message which would have to remain relevant through the centuries.

Interestingly enough, the writers of the Bible did not themselves always understand the full implications of what they wrote. Peter tells us, for example, that

> Concerning this salvation, the prophets, who spoke of the grace that was to come to you, searched intently and with the greatest care, trying to find out the time and circumstances to which the Spirit of Christ in them was pointing when he predicted the sufferings of Christ and the glories that would follow. It was revealed to them that they were not serving themselves but you, when they spoke of the things that have now been told you by those who have preached the gospel to you by the Holy Spirit sent from heaven. Even angels long to look into these things.[3]

The Holy Spirit gave inspired words to the Bible writers, not only for the original readers, but also for us today. Whether or not we can always identify it, surely a "faith that was once for all entrusted to the saints"[4] was given in a time and place deemed to be perfect for the future perpetuation of its timeless message.

The Problem of Discernment

That said, however, it simply can't be stressed enough that God anticipated cultural change. Had God wanted a church bound to the culture of the first century, no doubt we would have been given specific rules and regulations like those which were given to the Israelites in the wilderness— nothing but "thou shalts" and "thou shalt nots." The fact that we have principles and precedents, instead, is the clearest possible indication that God has given us an authoritative guide that is sufficiently flexible to fit in with any culture, time, or place.

If there are areas in which we must be wary of culture, there are also areas in which we must be sensitive to it.

Getting the balance is the key. But *how* to get the balance may be the surprise.

Paul told the Romans that cultural conformity is to be controlled from within. "Do not conform any longer to the pattern of this world," said Paul, "but be transformed by the renewing of your mind. Then you will be able to test and approve what God's will is—his good, pleasing and perfect will."[5] Getting the right balance is not a matter of cheap compromise and gratuitous accommodation, but naturally results from minds that are obedient to God's leading.

Spiritual Principles and Human Commands

Over the months of writing this book, I've wondered a lot about what it is that lies behind the desire for a cultural church. Is it nothing more than our unwittingly being absorbed into the secular world of which we are a part? I'm not so sure. Although cultural absorption is always a threat, my guess is that part of the explanation is found in our reaction to what at times has been the church's stifling traditionalism. As with most revolutions, we react out of circumstances of appalling spiritual barrenness.

Some years back, I lost my cool while visiting a congregation in which I had grown up. The adult Bible class was plodding along in a study book more geared to teenagers than the mature Christians who were in the class. The questions were not "thought questions," calling for serious reflection and discussion, but "feedback questions," asking only for the regurgitation of the same basic Bible facts that these Christians had learned as children.

All of a sudden, I found myself in the middle of a spirited tirade, rebuking a shocked group of people whom I know and love like family. Looking through the eyes of a "visitor," I was seeing what they had not seen—a lifetime of stagnation in the Word—and I just couldn't remain silent. Had I said nothing, "the stones would have cried out!"

It wasn't the class really. It was the memory. I remembered how we had preached sermons and taught lessons which had never quite captured the sublime message of the gospel. In fact, I remembered how we had taken powerful spiritual principles and emptied them of their power by enacting our own human legislation. We had taken the important principle of modesty, for example, and legislated the length of skirts. We had preached the important principle of chaste behavior, yet gone on to legislate the sin of dancing (whether lascivious dancing or folk dancing).

What we had done was to isolate ourselves from culture, fearful of being caught up in the principles of this world. But what an irony! When Paul warned the Colossians about "the basic principles of this world," he was not referring to the accommodative cultural church, but to the *traditional* church. Look at that amazing passage once again:

> Since you died with Christ to the basic principles of this world, why, as though you still belonged to it, do you submit to its rules: "Do not handle! Do not taste! Do not touch!"? These are all destined to perish with use, because they are based on human commands and teachings. Such regulations indeed have an appearance of wisdom, with their self-imposed worship, their false humility and their harsh treatment of the body, but they lack any value in restraining sensual indulgence.[6]

Who ever would have guessed that a fellowship priding itself in having the authority of *divine* commands could actually be perpetuating *human* commands! But what else is it when we legislate *mandatory applications* of biblical principles?

Proof that we were issuing "human commands" became self-evident. With each change in fashion and style, the "proper length" of the skirts kept shrinking higher and higher. Thanks to changing social expectations, even the traditional church had become the cultural church! Whereas biblical principles point to the *transcendent*, "human commands" are always culture-bound.

The call in this book to seek out and follow biblical "principles" is in direct contrast to what Paul describes as "the basic principles of this world." Human regulations reflect human principles which can taint even the most conservative elements of our fellowship. It's *God's* principles we must preach—not our own.

But If I Had to Choose...

Throughout this book, I have referred to a number of ironies regarding our fellowship. (Indeed, we are a curious—and altogether lovable—bunch of folks!) But one of the most disturbing ironies about us is that today's "cultural church" prides itself in being more *spiritual* and *holy*, when (at least to my observation) it's the more traditional congregations—with all their so-called legalism—which appear to *live* more morally upright.

I may be dead wrong about that, but just listen to the sermons that are preached in the "cultural church." Has anyone heard much about *sin* lately? Or *God's wrath*? How about *modesty* or *sobriety*? (If your experience is different, count yourself fortunate.) Judging from the way we sometimes show up for our services, the notion of modesty appears to be lost on us even at times of worship. Considering our casual disregard of spiritual principles, "human commands" look better by the minute!

If I had to choose between the "cultural church" and a church which tends toward legalism, I'm not sure which would get the nod. Take the matter of drinking, for instance. If the alternative to total abstinence is the increasing incidence of alcohol abuse witnessed among the more cultural churches in our fellowship, then give me total abstinence!

Having acknowledged that traditionalism can reflect its own brand of culturalism, it must be said that what marks the "cultural church" is not only culturally-influenced theology but also culturally-influenced moral values and standards. In a culture which is both immoral and increasingly amoral, we need *more* "moral support," not *less.*

I know whereof I speak. To use Paul's words, I am the chiefest of sinners. My concern is not just academic argument, but a daily personal struggle against my sinful self and a godless culture that entices me, lures me, and then derides my every effort at holiness. Not one of us is immune from its onslaught. In this godless environment, the last thing we need is a cultural church that has sold out to a cheap version of "morals by media."

Living Counter-Culture

In this regard, I have gained added appreciation for a whole new part of the sacred canon. In preparation for the writing of this book, I went back and carefully re-read the Bible, looking for anything resembling "commands," "examples," "principles," and "rules." In Acts and the Epistles, especially, I collected a large body of scriptures which were uniquely propositional, but not exactly what we might call "commands."

The headings that soon appeared on my computer screen were "Enumerated Virtues" and "Enumerated Vices." Under each heading were some thirty specific virtues and vices, many of which appeared again and again from one passage to another. Love, joy, peace, patience, and kindness—among many other virtues—are squared off in Scripture against such listed sins as drunkenness, sexual immorality, and filthy language.

I confess I'm not exactly sure where these "lists" fit in with the not-so-new hermeneutic of *purpose, principle, and precedent*. Certainly, the overarching principle of holiness leads us to seek the virtuous and shun the sinful. Therefore, I suppose we are still within the scope of stated "principles." But whatever the proper hermeneutical label, I am impressed by the specific attention given to each virtue and each vice. And all the more so, given the challenge which the cultural church faces in a society which has radically redefined what is "virtue" and what is "vice."

If we are to be a church in culture but not of culture, it will mean being *morally* Christ-centered as well as *doctrinally* Christ-centered. "Watch [both] your *life* and *doctrine* closely," Paul warned Timothy.[7]

Today's call for renewed spirituality will have to stand the test of true holiness. The church that is intolerant of traditionalism and legalism, but tolerant of divorce, sexual immorality, immodesty, and the dangers of alcohol has lost its mandate for either doctrinal or hermeneutical reform.

Oh, To Be Wrong!

As we come to the close of this book, it may seem odd but I can't help hoping that I am proved wrong in my concerns about what I have described as the "cultural church." My greatest joy would be to discover that my concerns are unfounded; that we are not being influenced by our culture in the radical way that I think we are.

On the other hand, even if I am right about where we are headed unless we are extremely careful, I would be elated some day to have egg all over my bearded face! If at the turn of the century I could look back and see that "the cultural church" changed its thinking in midstream and came back, I wouldn't mind for a moment looking absolutely silly for having predicted a parade of the horribles that never came to pass.

What I think I know even now is that it is not too late for us to rethink and regroup. As a fellowship, we've already got more going for us than most fellowships ever had, which is a determined commitment to biblical authority.

While we are tempted to downplay the significance of baptism, the denominational world is once again beginning to baptize! While we are somewhat embarrassed by our lack of any formal organization, the most vibrant churches in the land are those locally-autonomous "community churches" which don't even have the extensive "brotherhood" ties that we have.

While we are starting to experiment with "high church styles" and production numbers in worship, others are exploring the idea of simple gatherings without the need of formalistic ceremony or a professional clergy. And just when we are about to give up on traditional methods of Bible study, Evangelical churches from shore to shore are starting to dig back into "book, chapter, and verse." (Consider, for example, the newly-published International *Inductive* Study Bible!)

There's no reason to be embarrassed about our roots or threatened by our future as long as we stay the course. In the main, the call for a new hermeneutic reflects more *reaction* than *action.* My fear is that it may be more *deconstruction* than *reconstruction.* If there is a time for tearing down, there is also a time for building up. And, given the extraordinary challenge of our current culture, that time is now.

As for the not-so-new hermeneutic of *purpose, principle, and precedent,* I commit it to God in trust—prayerful that if it is faithful to his leading it may be a blessing to our better understanding of the unfathomable mystery of godliness.

DISCUSSION QUESTIONS

Chapter 1 — At the Crossroads

1. In your opinion, is the church having an identity crisis? If so, describe what you feel is causing it.
2. Are there any changes you would like to see made in the church today? If so, discuss.
3. Are current calls for change motivated by a renewed study of Scripture; by a desire for greater spirituality; by cultural change; or perhaps something else?
4. What is your understanding of the meaning of "hermeneutics"?
5. Before reading this chapter, were you familiar with "command, example, and necessary inference"? (Evaluate your group's degree of familiarity, considering the backgrounds of class members—e.g., age, gender, length of association with the churches of Christ.)
6. Have you heard any of the discussion aimed at bringing about a new hermeneutic? If so, discuss your understanding of what that discussion is all about.
7. In what ways do we sometimes act from two quite different motivations—both good and bad?
8. Give some examples of how we can be affected by our culture without being aware of it.
9. In what ways do you think the church is being affected by today's culture?
10. From reading the first chapter, what do you expect to get out of this study?

Chapter 2 — When Hermeneutics First Hit Home

1. Whether or not you grew up in the church, what were your first impressions as to how Scripture should be interpreted and applied?
2. If you have been familiar with the hermeneutic of "command, example, and necessary inference," how would you rate its effectiveness in determining Christian doctrine and practice?

3. How confident is your understanding of what it means to follow biblical "commands, examples, and necessary inferences"?

4. How consistent do you think the church has been in attempting to follow the New Testament pattern in our own time?

5. Suppose that there were no such thing as a formal hermeneutic. How do you think you would approach the interpretation and application of Scripture?

6. What do you think explains how two different Christians sharing the same basic hermeneutic can come to opposite views as to what the Scriptures teach on a given matter?

7. What, if any, have been your experiences with controversy and division among Christians, caused by differences in the way Scriptures are interpreted and applied?

8. What attitude do you think Christians ought to have toward each other when, after diligent and honest study, they differ in their understanding of Scripture?

9. Under what circumstances might differences in understanding necessitate having to worship apart from those with whom you differ?

10. If worshipping separately is ever thought to be necessary, what attitude do you think Christians on both sides ought nevertheless to have toward one another?

Chapter 3 — In Praise of the Old Hermeneutic

1. If our hermeneutic is a statement of faith, what is that statement?

2. Is our hermeneutic different from human creeds? If so, how?

3. On what does our hermeneutic (when properly applied) focus our attention?

4. What role does the "pattern principle" play in Scripture?

5. In what ways have we used the biblical pattern to shape the work and worship of the church?

6. In what ways have we used the biblical pattern to guide our lives to greater holiness?

7. Have we been more willing to use biblical pattern as a constitution for church doctrine than as a model for personal holiness?

8. In what way is Jesus himself a "hermeneutic"?

9. Have we transformed an honorable hermeneutic into an excuse for maintaining our own traditions?

10. Do you think the church would be any different if we were to abandon the "old hermeneutic"? If so, in what way?

Chapter 4 — Book, Chapter, and *Verse*

1. As we look back to our particular roots, what motivations lay behind the movement for restoration of the New Testament church?
2. In what ways did our concern for countering denomination-alism shape our thought and practice as a fellowship?
3. Is there a difference between the goal of restoring New Testament Christianity and defending the faith by denouncing denominational teaching? If so, describe that difference.
4. With what part of the New Testament are you more familiar—the Gospels, or Acts and the Epistles?
5. In your own congregation, which seems to be the emphasis—the core gospel or church doctrine?
6. What has been your experience with methods of study? Has it been primarily topical or expository? How do the two compare?
7. Is proof-texting a dying art? Should it be?
8. What are the advantages and disadvantages of verse-by-verse studies?
9. It's been suggested that we have overly-formalized the "name" of the church and the typical ending of our prayers. Do you agree? Can you think of any other instances in which we have been guilty of over-formalizing?
10. Can you think of any individual verses which have been taken out of their proper context and applied in ways never originally intended?

Chapter 5 — Changing Times, Changing Issues

1. What do you consider to be the top two or three most crucial social issues of our time?
2. What does the Bible have to say about those issues?
3. If the Bible says nothing directly about those issues, does it say anything about other matters which might affect the issues themselves?
4. What, if any, non-Christian religion have you come into contact with recently, and how have you used the Bible to confront its claims?

5. Is "command, example, and necessary inference" of help to you in resolving today's social issues or confronting other religions?

6. Which would more likely be discussed in your congregation: Instrumental music or abortion? Infant baptism or euthanasia? Dancing or the distribution of condoms in public schools? Divorce and remarriage or homosexuality?

7. Do you think that our particular hermeneutic has any impact on the kinds of topics we address as Christians?

8. Has there been any preaching or teaching in your congregation on New Age thinking or other modern heresies?

9. How can we use our hermeneutic to appeal to a biblically illiterate generation that rejects the authority of Scripture?

10. Does our hermeneutic tie us to the past, or prepare us for the future?

Chapter 6 — "New Hermeneutic"—A Ship Without Anchor

1. In what way is the "new morality" radically different from what we know as "moral decline"?

2. What is "utilitarian morality" and in what way is a "utilitarian hermeneutic" like it?

3. What are the key features of today's "political correctness" movement?

4. In what ways, if at all, do you see yourself altering your ideas or actions in order to be seen as more tolerant to people whose beliefs or lifestyles you might disapprove of?

5. In what ways can you see the church today being affected by cultural influences like the "new morality," "political correctness," and utilitarian thinking?

6. What factors have most influenced your own thinking regarding the role of women in the church? Biblical teaching? Cultural expectations? Your own sense of fairness? Something else?

7. Is there any matter of church doctrine with which you so strongly disagree that you sometimes wish you could simply ignore what you know the Bible teaches about it? Have you ever caught yourself actually doing it?

8. How would you explain for someone else the call for a new hermeneutic?

9. What risks do you see if our fellowship turns to some "new

hermeneutic"? What risks if we *don't?*

10. What do you think about the future of our fellowship? Where are we headed?

Chapter 7 — Rationalizing the Irrational

1. What role does our human logic play in the pursuit of spiritual truth?
2. What role does intuition play in our life of faith?
3. If either, which of the two—logic or intuition—is more important in our Christian walk?
4. Can you think of any biblical examples where human logic failed to meet the test of God?
5. Can you think of any biblical examples where abandoning divine law led God's people astray?
6. Can you cite biblical examples where rationalistic law-keeping became spiritually counterproductive?
7. As between logic and intuition, how would you describe the "spirit of our age"?
8. How can a rational hermeneutic (like "command, example, and necessary inference") be used irrationally?
9. How can a spiritually-sounding hermeneutic (a "hermeneutic of the cross," for example) be used unspiritually?
10. What role might pride play in the use of either the "old hermeneutic" or perhaps some "new hermeneutic"?

Chapter 8 — Looking At Others To See Ourselves

1. What does it tell us when we see other churches struggling with many of the same issues we are facing?
2. What invariably seems to be associated with changes in the way a given fellowship perceives the authority of the Bible?
3. Why is it that many fellowships have felt the need to abandon the Bible as the final word on God's truth?
4. Have you seen the idea of pluralism at work in the church? Was it for good or for ill?
5. What "gratuitous accommodation," if any, have you witnessed in the church?
6. In what way does the call for pluralism actually end up demanding conformity?
7. What "doctrinal beards" have we trimmed in order to be less conspicuous to the secular or religious world around us?

8. What lessons can we learn from what we know about early Jewish reformers in Germany?
9. How would you describe culture's own hermeneutic?
10. In what way does "pattern theology" prevent us from conforming to the world?

Chapter 9 — Enlightenment Rationality—An Unlikely Bogeyman

1. To what extent do we all face a temptation to adapt the message of Scripture to our own tastes or desires?
2. In what ways has "command, example, and necessary inference" been used to justify culture-bound beliefs in the past?
3. In what ways is the rejection of "command, example, and necessary inference" a product of the same phenomenon (justifying culture-bound beliefs of our day)?
4. What are the respective advantages and disadvantages of approaching the Bible with what might be called scientific method or inductive reasoning?
5. In what various ways can biblical "facts" be considered helpful in our pursuit of God?
6. What are some of the principle differences between "command, example, and necessary inference" and Enlightenment thinking? What similarities?
7. With what would your approach to the Bible be more closely associated: intellectual and logical or emotional and intuitive?
8. What role does common sense play in your own understanding of the Bible?
9. Deism is the belief that God acted once (in Creation) but no longer involves himself in the affairs of man. Is there any sense in which that deistic perspective might be shared in the church today?
10. Do you think our nation and its government would have been significantly different if there had more or fewer Deists involved in the writing of its early documents?

Chapter 10 — Narrative, Myth, and Metaphor

1. How have you most often thought of the Bible—as a story, or as a collection of rules and regulations?
2. Have you ever read the Bible story from cover to cover? If so,

did it change your perspective on the meaning of Scripture?

3. Why is the telling of stories so valuable to us?
4. What might we miss if we obey God's explicit commands without concentrating on the divine story?
5. Might one kind of hermeneutic be better for some parts of the Bible, while other kinds are more suitable elsewhere? Which kind best fits each part?
6. In what ways can we benefit from biblical metaphors, like *Christ* as *King*, or the *church* as *kingdom*?
7. What dangers lie in the use of a "narrative hermeneutic"?
8. In what ways can the idea of story be abused?
9. What lessons can we learn from Islamic scholars about common sense and metaphorical interpretation?
10. If Alexander Campbell and Joseph Campbell were to sit down together and read Acts chapter 2, how do you think they might interpret it?

Chapter 11 — Purpose, Principle, and Precedent

1. What is encompassed in the pursuit of *exegesis*? How might it differ in some respects from *hermeneutics*?
2. What kinds of questions are suggested by Who, What, When, Where, and Why?
3. What dangers do we face if we fail to look for "purpose" when trying to apply the Scriptures for today?
4. What advantages might there be in focusing on "principles" rather than "commands"?
5. Can you think of any ways in which "commands" actually better serve our efforts at interpretation?
6. Are there any dangers in thinking of "principles" rather than "commands"?
7. What is the essential difference between "examples" and "precedent"?
8. How can we decide what is merely a biblical occurrence and what is an authoritative example?
9. Can you think of any passages where we have confused "commands" and "examples," or instances in which we have found "commands" or "examples" where neither was intended?
10. If you were asked to come up with a hermeneutic that would enable you to better interpret Scripture, what might it be?

Chapter 12 — Applying the Not-So-New Hermeneutic

1. There may be yet another analogy from driving in fog. What lesson might we see, for instance, in the difference between using our high beams and low beams?
2. What scriptures can you think of that might further illustrate the importance of *the coherence factor?*
3. In what ways could our understanding of Scripture be enhanced by making it more Christ-centered?
4. What caution must be exercised when using a "Jesus grid" to filter our understanding of scriptures?
5. What role do you see the Holy Spirit playing in our search for spiritual insight?
6. In what ways (and with what frequency) do you actively invoke God's leading through your prayers?
7. What is your understanding of the relationship between principles and rules?
8. If there are apparent conflicts between various spiritual principles, how do you resolve those conflicts?
9. Are there any principles or precedents which you think are being "overruled," practically speaking, either in your local congregation or in our fellowship at large?
10. Can you think of instances in which we have made wrong choices in the doctrinal smorgasbord of biblical examples?

Chapter 13 — The Deafening Roar of Biblical Silence

1. In what way does "the argument from silence" go hand in hand with a "back-to-the-Bible" hermeneutic?
2. What dangers accompany the use of arguments based on the silence of the Scripture?
3. Is the matter of church music a good illustration of "the argument from silence"? Why?
4. Relative to instrumental music, do you think we have forced too much out of the "silence" of Ephesians 5:19 and Colossians 3:16?
5. What is the difference between an "aid to worship" and an "addition to worship"?
6. What do you feel is the reason that some within the churches of Christ are calling for use of musical instruments?
7. Why do we seem to honor the silence of Scripture for some

things, but not for others? (For example, song books, church buildings, and four-part harmony.)

8. Can you think of illustrations, other than church music, where the silence of Scripture might be important?

9. What questions should we ask ourselves before using the argument from silence to determine how we should proceed in matters of faith and worship?

10. In what two radically different ways do people approach the silence of Scripture, and what perspectives might they reflect?

Chapter 14 — Cultural Church, Or Church in Culture?

1. What is there about our worship that is scripturally neutral and simply reflects our American or other local culture?

2. Is there anything that we do as a church that is culturally suspect and without the backing of Scripture?

3. In what ways might we need to be more culturally sensitive without abandoning biblical authority?

4. Have we accepted anything into our worship simply because it is trendy or faddish?

5. In what ways has traditionalism or legalism also ended up being culturally driven?

6. Do you think that the biblical pattern would be significantly different had Christ come into the world at a different time and in another culture? Is it important that Jesus came when and where he did?

7. How does your own congregation stack up when it comes to the correlation between doctrine and holiness?

8. What is your overall response to the call for a new hermeneutic?

9. What is your evaluation of *purpose, principle, and precedent* as a hermeneutic?

10. How, if at all, has this study helped you to gain a better understanding of the Bible, and, more importantly, the God of the Bible?

REFERENCES

Chapter 1 — *At the Crossroads*

Chapter 2 — *When Hermeneutics First Hit Home*

1. 2 Timothy 1:13.
2. Jude 1:3.
3. Exodus 32:1-35.
4. 2 Samuel 6:6-11; 1 Chronicles 13:9-14.
5. Leviticus 10: 1-3.
6. Luke 11: 37-52.
7. 1 Timothy 3:15.
8. Matthew 28:19.
9. Romans 16:16; Corinthians 16:20; 2 Corinthians 13:12; 1 Thessalonians 5:26.
10. Acts 2:42; 20:7; 1 Corinthians 10:16-21; 11:20-34.
11. Matthew 4:2; Acts 9:9; 13:3; 14:23.
12. Mark 6:5; 7:32; 16:18; Luke 4:40; Acts 19:6; 1 Timothy 4:14; 2 Timothy 1:6.
13. Acts 17:11.
14. Acts 17:16-21.
15. Genesis 2:17.

Chapter 3 — *In Praise of the Old Hermeneutic*

1. Thomas Campbell and Thomas Acheson, *Declaration and Address* (1809).
2. 2 Timothy 1:13.
3. Exodus 25:9.
4. Hebrews 8:1-2.
5. Hebrews 8:5.
6. 2 Timothy 1:13.
7. 2 Timothy 3:16-17.
8. Philippians 3:17.
9. 1 Peter 2:21.
10. 1 Corinthians 11:1.
11. John 1:14.

12. John 1:18.
13. Matthew 28:19-20; Mark 16:15-16.
14. Acts 2:41; 8:36-39; 10:48; 19:5.
15. Galatians 3:27.

Chapter 4 — *Book, Chapter, and Verse*

1. Acts 2:47.
2. Acts 18:28.
3. Acts 9:2.
4. 1 Corinthians 1:2.
5. Romans 16:16.

Chapter 5 — *Changing Times, Changing Issues*

1. Acts 23:5.
2. Acts 17:22-31.
3. Proverbs 14:34.

Chapter 6 — *"New Hermeneutic"—A Ship Without Anchor*

1. Judges 21:25.
2. Numbers 3:4.
3. 2 Samuel 6:1-8.
4. Genesis 3:16.
5. Genesis 17:9-14.
6. Exodus 40:12-15.
7. Judges 4:1-5:31.
8. Acts 6:1-7.
9. 1 Corinthians 11:3.
10. Ephesians 5:22.
11. 1 Timothy 2:12.
12. 1 Corinthians 11:10.
13. 1 Timothy 2:14.
14. 1 Timothy 2:13.
15. Galatians 3:28.
16. Ephesians 5:21-6:9; Colossians 3:18-4:1.
17. Ephesians 5:21.
18. 1 Timothy 3:2.

Chapter 7 — *Rationalizing the Irrational*

1. Jeremiah 10:23.
2. Proverbs 14:12.
3. Proverbs 3:5-6.
4. Matthew 22:37; Deuteronomy 6:5.
5. Luke 24:45.
6. Romans 11:33-34.
7. Romans 16:26.
8. John 5:39.
9. John 16:13.
10. Hebrews 13:8.

Chapter 8 — *Looking At Others To See Ourselves*

1. *The Sunday Times* (London), in *Renewal*, July 1991, 7.
2. "Marxist Challenge in the City of Slums," *The Daily Telegraph* (London), 8 July 1991, 15.
3. "Churchgoing Is Growing on Saturday," *Los Angeles Times*, 21 Sept. 1991, F15.
4. "Letters," *Christianity Today*, 27 May 1991, 6.
5. James R. Edwards, "Eros Deified," *Christianity Today*, 27 May 1991, 14-15.
6. Hebrews 12:1.
7. Edwards, "Eros."
8. Matthew 19:3-12.
9. William G. Braude, "From the Point of View of History," in *Reform Judaism: A Historical Perspective*, ed. Joseph L. Blau (Hoboken: KTAV, 1973), 104.
10. Deuteronomy 17:14.
11. Ellis Rivkin, "Some Historical Aspects of Authority in Judaism," in *Reform Judaism*.
12. Michael A. Meyer, *Response to Modernity—A History of the Reform Movement in Judaism* (Oxford University Press, 1988), ix, 4-6, 8, 10, 12-14, 18, 29, 55.
13. Romans 12:2.

Chapter 9 — *Enlightenment Rationality—An Unlikely Bogeyman*

1. Hebrews 5:11.

2. Romans 2:14-15.
3. Alexander Campbell, *The Christian System* (Bethany, Virginia, 1839), 6.
4. John Locke, *The Reasonableness of Christianity* (1695), 5.
5. Ephesians 3:17-19.
6. Ephesians 1:18.
7. Ephesians 3:8-9.
8. John Locke, *An Essay Concerning Human Understanding* (1690), 4.18.3.
9. John Locke, *Mr. Locke's Reply to the Right Reverend the Bishop of Worcester's Answer to His Letter* (1697), 147, 275.
10. John W. Yolton, *Locke, An Introduction,* (Oxford: Basil Blackwell, 1985), 45.
11. See Locke's introduction to his *Paraphrases of St. Paul's Epistles* in *Works* (1823 edition), III, 21.
12. Locke, *Essay,* sec. 14.
13. 1 Corinthians 1:22-24.

Chapter 10 — *Narrative, Myth, and Metaphor*

1. Walter Fisher, *Human Communication As Narration: Toward a Philosophy of Reason, Value, and Action* (Columbia: University of South Carolina Press, 1987), 5, 63, 67.
2. John 15:12.
3. John 14:6.
4. J. Windrow Sweetman, *Islam and Christian Theology* (London: Lutterworth Press, 1967), 180-189.
5. Ibid.
6. Belden C. Lane, "The Power of Myth: Lessons from Joseph Campbell," *The Christian Century*, vol. 106, no. 21 (5-12 July, 1989), 652-654.
7. Ibid.
8. Betty Sue Flowers, ed., *Joseph Campbell, The Power of Myth, with Bill Moyers* (New York: Doubleday, 1988), 141-142, 148, 163.
9. Ibid.
10. Ibid.
11. Ibid.
12. Ibid.

13. Ibid.
14. John 1:1.
15. John 1:14.
16. Lane, "Power."

Chapter 11 — *Purpose, Principle, and Precedent*

1. 1 Corinthians 1:17.
2. 1 Corinthians 1:14.
3. 1 Corinthians 1:16.
4. Galatians 5:2.
5. Acts 16:1-3.
6. 1 Timothy 2:12.
7. Titus 2:3-4.
8. 2 Timothy 2:15.
9. 1 Timothy 3:14-15; 4:11.
10. 1 Corinthians 7:10.
11. 1 Corinthians 7:6.
12. 1 Corinthians 7:12.
13. 1 Corinthians 7:40.
14. 1 John 5:3-4.
15. Romans 16:16.
16. 2 Timothy 4:13.
17. 2 Timothy 4:21.
18. 1 Corinthians 11:16.
19. Matthew 10:42.
20. 2 Corinthians 8:8-11.
21. 1 Corinthians 16:2.
22. 2 Corinthians 8:20-21.
23. 1 Timothy 4:13, 16; 5:1, 23; 4:1-2, 5.
24. 1 Corinthians 2:13.
25. Luke 22:12.
26. Acts 18:18.
27. Acts 13:8-11.
28. Acts 2:44-45.
29. Acts 2:46.
30. 1 Corinthians 11:17-34.
31. 1 Timothy 5:9-10.
32. Timothy 5:17.
33. Acts 20:7.
34. Acts 14:14.

35. Luke 22:12.
36. Acts 10:1-48.
37. Matthew 28:19-20; Mark 16:15-16.
38. Acts 10:34-35.
39. Acts 11:17.
40. Matthew 28:19.
41. Acts 2:38.

Chapter 12 — *Applying the Not-So-New Hermeneutic*

1. Acts 2:44-45.
2. 1 Corinthians 7:17.
3. 1 Corinthians 14:33-34, 37.
4. 1 Samuel 15:22.
5. Micah 6:8.
6. John 4:20-21.
7. John 8:1-11.
8. Matthew 21:12-13; Mark 11:15-17; Luke 19:45-46.
9. Matthew 5:22; 23:15.
10. Matthew 16:13.
11. Acts 2:38.
12. Ephesians 3:16.
13. Hebrews 4:12.
14. 2 Thessalonians 2:13.
15. Ephesians 1:17.
16. Ephesians 3:16.
17. Romans 8:26.
18. Hebrews 1:1-2.

Chapter 13 — *The Deafening Roar of Biblical Silence*

1. Galatians 5:1.
2. Deuteronomy 12:32.
3. 1 Corinthians 4:6.
4. Hebrews 8:1-5.
5. Hebrews 7:11-12.
6. Hebrews 9:6-14; 10:1-18.
7. Hebrews 8:13.
8. Amos 6:5; 1 Kings 10:12; Psalm 150:4; Habakkuk 3:19;
   2 Chronicles 29:27.
9. 1 Chronicles 23:5.
10. *Catholic Encyclopedia*, 1913 ed., s.v. "Musical."

11. Ephesians 4:1-5:20
12. Colossians 3:1-16
13. In the past, we have used Ephesians 5:19 and Colossians 3:16 as the primary scriptural authority for our argument from silence on the matter of instrumental music. However, given the requirement that silence must be *intended* in order to be authoritative, serious reconsideration is in order as to what these specific passages were meant to convey.

Perhaps an illustration can help us see more clearly the proper use of these two passages. Suppose that a father were to say to his teenage son, "Son, take the Ford Saturday night." If there were two cars in the garage—one a Ford, the other a Cadillac—everyone would understand that the father was intending his silence about the Cadillac to be controlling. In directing the son to drive the Ford, the father necessarily excluded use of the Cadillac. But now suppose that the father said to his son, "When you drive the car, drive carefully." From that statement alone, no one would assume any indication as to the father's intention regarding which of the two cars should be driven.

Given their context, Ephesians 5:19 and Colossians 3:16 are more like the second statement than the first. Neither passage specifically directs singing as a matter of Christian worship, as if, on one hand, to authorize singing while, on the other, excluding instrumental music. Both passages *assume* singing is already a part of the worship of the church and refer to it tangentially in connection with the believer's transformed life. Like the father saying to his son: "When you drive, drive carefully," Paul told first-century Christians: "Let the word of Christ dwell in you richly as you teach and admonish one another with all wisdom, and as you sing psalms, hymns, and spiritual songs with gratitude in your hearts to God."

Had Paul said, "When you worship, I want you to preach the gospel, pray, take the Lord's supper, and sing," then there would be a stronger case for intended silence ruling out the use of instruments. It would have been more like the father saying to his son, "Son, take the Ford Saturday night." Where one form of worship is *intentionally and specifically enjoined*, then all other forms are properly excluded. But that is not the nature of either Ephesians 5:19 or Colossians 3:16.

We simply have no import license to make of these passages more than is legitimately there. In context, neither passage satisfies the two requirements for applying the authority of silence. Because their primary purpose is not specifically to enjoin church singing, neither passage is intended to be either permissive or prohibitive of the kind of music which is authorized.

Unfortunately, there are some in the church today who point to our traditional use of Ephesians 5:19 and Colossians 3:16 as strong support for a new hermeneutic. "If forced doctrinal teaching is what you get from the 'old hermeneutic,'" we are being told, "then the 'old hermeneutic' ought to be abandoned."

One of the best pieces of advice I pass along to my trial practice students is *never use a weak argument.* In our eagerness to throw everything we've got into the fray, we usually end up giving our opponent something vulnerable to exploit. Once he sees a weak spot, all he has to do is to capitalize on it and the jury will quickly forget the stronger arguments.

If we abuse the context of specific passages when trying to extract scriptural authority for the work and worship of the church, we open the door for anyone wanting either to introduce some novel innovation or to call for some radical new way of understanding the Bible. Is that what we want to do? The good news, as we have seen, is that we don't have to.

Rather than being upset that we have pressed certain passages into service for a purpose they were never intended to serve, we should be excited to gain a fresh appreciation for the real message they were intended to convey. Who among us doesn't need encouragement to live more joyous, holy, and Spirit-filled lives in Christ?

As for musical instruments in Christian worship, the silence of the entire New Testament text is more than sufficient warrant for their exclusion. The silence is both intended and resounding!

Chapter 14 — *Cultural Church, or Church in Culture?*

1. Acts 2:6.
2. 1 Corinthians 5:9-10.
3. 1 Peter 1:10-12.
4. Jude 3.
5. Romans 12:2.
6. Colossians 2:20-23.
7. 1 Timothy 4:16.